YNAMIC DUO
ierre
Jim
ierre:
ou light up
my life!
TRUDEAU:
FOR
STRONG
GOVERNMENT

Trudeau Albums

PENGUIN
STUDIO

AN
OTHERWISE INC.
EDITION

Trudeau Albums was produced by Otherwise Inc. Editions

Editorial and art direction Sara Borins
Design and typesetting 52 Pick-up Inc., Toronto
Editors Karen Alliston, Rick Archbold, Jennifer Glossop, Alison Maclean, Ivon Owen
Editorial assistance and research Tom Berkhout, Jennifer Heyns, Sarah Webster
Captions Tom Berkhout

Otherwise Inc. Editions offers special thanks to Serge Allaire, Derek Berkhout, Judy Biggar, Guy Borrmans, Stephen Bulger, Duncan Cameron, Stevie Cameron, Jean-Marc Carisse, Dean Cooke, Catherine Dean, Jean Demers, Bill Douglas, Greig Dymond, Andrea Fitzgerald, Cynthia Good, Andrea Gordon, Linda Griffiths, Kevin Hanson, David Hermans, Jackie Kaiser, Sue Lagasi, Jean Lauzon, Jerry Levitan, Avi Lewis, Stephen Lyons, Jean Matheson, Susan McIntee, Nick Monteleone, Phil Norton, Charles Pachter, Chris Pommer, Kelly Pullen, Ian Rapsey, Bree Seeley, Crawford Smith, Gabor Szilasi, Paula Thiessen, George S. Zimbel.

Penguin Studio
Published by the Penguin Group
Penguin Books Canada Ltd, 10 Alcorn Avenue, Toronto, Ontario, Canada M4V 3B2
Penguin Books Ltd, 27 Wrights Lane, London W8 5TZ, England
Penguin Putnam Inc., 375 Hudson Street, New York, New York 10014, U.S.A.
Penguin Books Australia Ltd, Ringwood, Victoria, Australia
Penguin Books (NZ) Ltd, cnr Rosedale and Airborne Roads, Albany, Auckland 1310, New Zealand

Penguin Books Ltd, Registered Offices: Harmondsworth, Middlesex, England

First published 2000

10 9 8 7 6 5 4 3 2 1

Canadian Cataloguing in Publication Data
Main entry under title:
Trudeau albums
ISBN 0-670-89293-9

1. Trudeau, Pierre Elliott, 1919-   .   2. Trudeau, Pierre Elliott, 1919-   - Portraits.
3. Prime ministers – Canada – Biography.   4. Prime ministers – Canada – Portraits.
I. Borins, Sara. II. Gzowski, Peter.

FC626.T7T782 2000   971.064'4'092   C00-931053-3
F1034.3.T7T775 2000

Printed and bound in Canada on acid free paper

Visit Penguin Canada's web site at **www.penguin.ca**

Produced by
Otherwise Inc. Editions
356A Queen Street West
Toronto ON M5V 2A2

The Contrarian 1919 to 1949

Into Power 1949 to 1968

p.36

Watch Me 1968 to 1974

p.64

Domestic Malaise
1974 to 1980

p.88

I'm Back
1980 to 1984

p.118

The Sphinx
1984 to 2000

p.138

The Contrarian
1919 to 1949

The Contrarian | Jack Granatstein

T HE STORY HAS ALMOST ASSUMED THE quality of a hallowed myth. The child is born of a French-Canadian father and a Scottish-Canadian mother in 1919; born into a family soon to be very wealthy. The boy, frail in his youth, develops his mind and his body by sheer force of will. Early on, his contrarian spirit develops and he tests himself in solitary journeys around the globe, and in intellectual efforts in Montreal, at Harvard University, at the Sorbonne, and at the London School of Economics. Then, a different test in tussles with the authoritarian regime of Quebec Premier Maurice Duplessis.

But, unlike most myths, this story of Pierre Trudeau's formation is almost all true. Almost, but not quite. To me, the often-told tale neglects the most important parts of the pre-public career of one of this country's great prime ministers. Pierre Trudeau has said repeatedly that the only consistency in his life is that he has always opposed the prevailing ideas and resisted the received opinions of his times. (A collection of his writings, for example, is called *Against the Current.*) Certainly this is true of his animosity towards Duplessis and his long war against nationalism and separatism from the late 1950s onward. But when did the trait emerge? When was it that Pierre Trudeau developed his attitude of going against the grain?

In truth, there was little sign of this habit of mind in his youth. He loved his father and adored his mother, communicating easily in French and English at home. His father made his millions by developing a chain of gas stations and an automobile service association that took shrewd advantage of the boom in car ownership in the 1920s, and the family lived very well through the Great Depression. There were lazy summer holidays and European vacations and a pervasive Roman Catholicism. The comfort and contentment ended with the sudden death of his father when Pierre was fifteen.

Pierre Trudeau attended the best francophone school in Montreal, the Collège Jean-de-Brébeuf, a Jesuit-run *collège classique* that honed his mind. Certainly, there were signs of a smartass attitude, of a sharp tongue that made up for his still-frail body, stories of his puncturing the pomposity of teachers and savaging student colleagues. But there was nothing in his infrequent school newspaper articles truly to suggest a contrarian streak. In fact, when he wrote it was about skiing or canoeing, personal episodes that, while important in tracing his developing interests, his growing self-discipline, and his willingness to push himself to the limit, show little trace of the intellect that would later be so powerful.

Where politics was concerned, Trudeau claimed in his memoirs to have been totally uninterested. Politics was "a waste of time." He graduated from Collège Jean-de-Brébeuf in 1940 and went to the Université de Montréal in the fall of that year to study law. Canada was at war, France was occupied, and the Western world was in danger of falling under the Nazi heel. And Trudeau was indifferent? Parliament passed the National Resources Mobilization Act in June 1940 and national registration, seen in Quebec as a certain precursor of conscription, took place in

French Connection
In 1908, eleven years before Pierre Elliott Trudeau was born, Quebec celebrated the 300th anniversary of Samuel de Champlain's arrival in Quebec City and the founding of New France. Festivities included dressing up in costumes of the province's founders, including King Henry IV of France and Queen Mary, portrayed here by Monsieur A. Couillard and Madame Auguste Carrier. The anniversary ceremonies reminded French Canadians of their unique heritage and their links to France. Following Britain's victory on the Plains of Abraham in 1759, the habitants of New France were deserted by the French ruling class, save for the Catholic Church.

August 1940. Montreal Mayor Camillien Houde, calling on his compatriots to resist registration, was incarcerated at Camp Petawawa, and Trudeau was uninterested? At university, male students were urged to join the Canadian Officers Training Corps, and biographers suggest that Trudeau was enough of a troublemaker that he was "kicked out for lack of discipline." Ordinarily, such an action would have been followed by immediate call-up for military service under the terms of the National Resources Mobilization Act, but Trudeau somehow managed to escape this by joining the reserve battalion of Les Fusiliers Mont-Royal. And still he was uninterested? Are we to assume his interest was not aroused by the unpleasant prospect that he might be made to join the nation's active forces? Like other regiments, Les Fusiliers Mont-Royal in August 1942 had suffered terrible losses in the abortive raid on Dieppe. And Trudeau remained unconcerned? "I was bored by the *present*," he said later of those wartime years.

If so, he was very much like most Québécois who viewed the war as a British imperialist struggle of little interest to Canada as a whole, and even less to French Canada. Yes, 150,000 francophones served in the Canadian forces during the Second World War, roughly three times as many as had served during the Great War. But there is little doubt that lack of interest or, worse, opposition to the war was very common. In the spring of 1942, with Japan now in the war and the Canadian West Coast in danger of attack, with Nazi U-boats sinking ships in the Gulf of St. Lawrence, the Liberal government of W.L. Mackenzie King staged a plebiscite with the object of securing release from its repeated promises against overseas conscription. After a strong campaign for a "Non" vote in Quebec, a huge French-Canadian majority refused King's request; but English Canadians across the nation voted heavily to give the government a free hand.

There is no record that Trudeau participated in the "Non" campaign or directly in La Ligue pour la défense du Canada, which was created to lead the anti-conscriptionist effort. He states in his memoirs that the government imposed conscription in 1942 (it didn't) so there seems little reason to doubt that he supported the Ligue's aims – like 80 percent of Québécois. Indeed, in the late autumn of 1942 he spoke at rallies for Jean Drapeau, the candidate of the *nationaliste* and anti-conscriptionist Bloc populaire Canadien in the Outremont by-election. On one occasion Trudeau's clever remarks made the front-page headline of *Le Devoir*. This gets no mention in his memoirs.

In other words, Trudeau was the opposite of a contrarian; he was, instead, at one with the majority. The contrarian Québécois were those who supported the war, who saw the Nazi threat to Canada and to freedom, and who, like the volunteers overseas with Les Fusiliers Mont-Royal, enlisted. Trudeau stood with those opposed to participation, opposed to conscription, and supportive of the collaborationist Vichy French regime of Marshal Philippe Pétain. The Abbé Groulxs and the André Laurendeaus were anti-British, pro-Vichy, and anti-conscriptionist. They were also viciously anti-Semitic. Happily, there is nothing to indicate that Trudeau shared this last trait. Nonetheless, it is indisputable that those he associated with, those he spoke for in the Outremont by-election, were the inward-looking *nationalistes* who had

Nationalist Divide

Sir Wilfrid Laurier, holding his hat on the campaign trail in Ontario (TOP), understood the nationalist divides that confronted his fledgling nation. Following his Liberal Party's defeat in the 1911 election, the impassioned politician stated, "I am branded in Quebec as a traitor to the French, in Ontario as a traitor to the English," a sentiment that would be well understood by the nation's subsequent prime ministers, in particular Pierre Elliott Trudeau.

At the turn of the century, the Quebec countryside (BOTTOM LEFT) fostered many French-Canadian families who followed the Catholic Church's vision of an honest and pious life spent tilling the fields. The society of French Canada was changing, however, from a rural-agricultural one to an urban-industrial one. Although his family had farmed the south bank of the St. Lawrence River for nine generations, Joseph Trudeau, Pierre Trudeau's grandfather, decided

that his children's future lay not in the country, but in the city. The Trudeau farm was sold, and the family moved to Montreal (BOTTOM RIGHT). Pierre's mother, Grace Trudeau, an anglophone, was familiar with Quebec's linguistic divide. As a Catholic, she was first educated in Montreal at a convent-school, then was placed in the bosom of English society at Dunham Ladies' College in the Eastern Townships.

completely misjudged world and Canadian events. Indeed, these people, these attitudes, were the very ones Trudeau would later oppose in his long crusade against *nationalisme* and separatism.

All that Trudeau says in his memoirs, and in the few interviews where he responded to queries on his attitudes and actions during the wartime years, is that he knew little of the issues involved. Somehow, this rings very hollow, and Trudeau's evident embarrassment in answering questions shows through. There is, as a present-day contrarian, historian Esther Delisle, has written, a conscious effort to forget the Second World War among the members of the Quebec elite. Trudeau, no contrarian at this time of his life, shares this stance.

Trudeau has said that it was not until he went to Harvard University in 1944 (after seeking the advice of the *nationalistes* icons Henri Bourassa and André Laurendeau!), his freshly minted law degree in hand, that he began to understand the war's importance. Presumably he had the permission of the National Selective Service that would have been required to allow a young, fit male reservist to leave Canada. The Americans were fighting, and they certainly were not doing so to support British imperialism. Some of his professors at Cambridge were refugees from Nazism, and the shortage of young men in his classes must have struck him forcibly. But again, at a time when he could have returned to Canada to enlist or even have signed up with the US forces (as war correspondent René Lévesque did), Trudeau confined himself to his studies, to confirming his developing "beliefs about individual freedom." As he said later, he slowly came to the realization that he had missed the great adventure of the century.

This realization and his dawning understanding of what the Nazis had done to Europe were reinforced by his travels to Paris and London in the immediate postwar years. The French had suffered terribly under the Nazis for four years and more; London had been blitzed, and there was scarcely a family in Western Europe that had not lost loved ones in battle, in bombings, or in concentration camps. His new comprehension must have made him question the views he had held, the men he had supported, and the policies he had spoken for in Montreal during the war. The contrarian Trudeau, I suggest, developed at the end of and after the Second World War.

Trudeau would later spend a year bumming around the globe and, when he returned in 1949, he was prepared to turn against the *nationaliste* establishment and to begin his opposition to the received wisdom of Quebec. Some others were making this turn, in whole or in part. André Laurendeau, the driving force behind La Ligue pour la défense du Canada and the Bloc populaire Canadien, remained anti-British and anti-Semitic, but he was against the Duplessis regime and the stifling power exercised by the Church. Trudeau found friends in young radicals like Gérard Pelletier and Jean Marchand and a cause in the struggle of the workers in the mining town of Asbestos. In his efforts, he was opposed by the Church, by the government, and by most right-thinking Québécois.

Whatever Trudeau might have been in the early 1940s, by the end of that decade he had begun to resemble the Trudeau all Canadians came to know after 1968.

The contrarian had taken form.

Political Birth

In 1919, at the end of World War I, Canada was a nation confronting nationalist issues, diplomatic loyalties, and political ideologies. Conscription, which demanded the military service of Canadian men during the latter part of the war, had inflamed the cultural split between French and English Canadians. The English viewed military service as a duty to England, Canada's mother country, as exemplified by the graffiti on the wall behind these war veterans (TOP). The French regarded World War I as an imperialist battle fought between European nations, in which they had no role.

The end of World War I saw thousands of Canadian soldiers, including these wounded men (BOTTOM LEFT), return from Europe to a country very different from the one they left. As leaders of the victorious Allied nations gathered at Versailles, France, the Canadian Prime Minister Robert Borden insisted that his country and the other dominions be separate signatories to the peace accord. The notion of Canada as a nation independent of England was officially introduced.

With the conclusion of one battle, the start of another began, this time between the rights of labour and the needs of free-market capitalism. Friction between the two combatants spilled onto the streets of Manitoba's capital during the late spring of 1919 in the Winnipeg General Strike (BOTTOM RIGHT). The six-week-long demonstration of labour unrest paralyzed the city and triggered a wave of short-lived strikes across the country. On October 18, 1919, against a backdrop of nascent issues that would fuel Canadian politics for the next century, Pierre Elliott Trudeau was born in Outremont, Quebec, a suburb of Montreal.

1925 | Boyhood

Go, Pierre

Until he was twelve years old, Pierre Trudeau lived at the north end of rue Durocher in Outremont, a bourgeois suburb of Montreal, where boys often doubled up for tricycle rides (BELOW). "My street," as Trudeau referred to rue Durocher, was a microcosm of the city itself. Catholics, Protestants, Jews, French Canadians, Irish, and Scots all lived there.

For the shy young Pierre, however, the street was not just a place for gentle play. Charles Trudeau, a supporter of Montreal's boxing scene (RIGHT), gave his physically petit son fighting lessons and introduced him to some of the city's most popular professional brawlers. With such training, Pierre was frequently chosen to represent rue Durocher's honour when a sparring challenge arose. His friends would cheer him, shouting, "Go on, Pierre! You can do it! Go on!"

Industrious Education

It was imperative for Charles Trudeau that his children receive a strong liberal education. He enrolled his sons, Pierre and Charles (nicknamed Tip), in Académie Querbes, a modern Catholic school that had opened in 1916. Attended by Montreal's wealthy French-Canadian and Irish Catholic communities, Querbes was an ideal school for the Trudeau sons. Governed by priests (LEFT), the institution offered classes in both French and English, allowing Charles to place his sons in English classes for the first three grades, before transferring them to lessons in French. Although Querbes was a multi-room academy, all the grades taught in English were conducted in a single classroom like the one shown below.

On entering the first grade, the young Pierre learned that his close companion Gerald O'Connor was sitting in the section of the room designated for the second-year students. Sensing an injustice, he convinced the principal to allow him to advance a grade to be in the same class as his friend. Thus, Pierre won the first of a long line of battles.

1928 | Montreal

First City

"Let the capital of England and of the United States come here as much as it wishes and multiply our industries, so that our people will have work," said Quebec Premier Louis-Alexandre Taschereau in October 1927. Throughout the decade foreign investment flowed into Quebec, with Montreal at its financial centre. The city expanded rapidly and Pierre Trudeau grew up in an urban society that enjoyed the luxuries of the Roaring Twenties. Abuzz with the sounds of jazz, the mesmerizing sight of transatlantic airships high in the sky (ABOVE), and the ringing of cash registers in its flourishing shopping districts (TOP RIGHT), Montreal was indisputably the country's first city in population, economic clout, and culture.

Prosperity and Politics

Shunned by the English elite of Quebec, the success of prosperous French Canadians during the 1920s, including Charles Trudeau, depended on entrepreneurial ambition and political allies. A long-standing Conservative "bleu," Charles Trudeau was friendly with Camillien Houde (RIGHT), the leader of the Quebec Conservative Party from 1928 to 1932, and Maurice Duplessis, an aspiring Quebec politician. The extroverted Charles frequently invited up to twenty of his friends to his home on Lac Tremblant in the summer. In the winter months, the same crowd gathered in the family's basement, where they vigorously discussed politics between card games and amid the clanging of glasses.

Recognizing the impact that the automobile would have on the twentieth century, Charles Trudeau built up a chain of garages and service stations like the one pictured here (OPPOSITE, BOTTOM LEFT). In 1932, he sold his flourishing business to Imperial Oil Limited for just over $1 million. The new capital allowed Charles to invest successfully in the Montreal Royals (OPPOSITE, BOTTOM RIGHT) and Belmont Amusement Park (OPPOSITE, TOP), entertaining ventures that closely paralleled his robust personality.

En Route

During the Great Depression, Canadians were divided dramatically by class. Half the population was employed and continuing to enjoy the comforts they had acquired in the 1920s, while the other half could not find work and desperately sought the means to survive. By the summer of 1931, the federal government had put $20 million into public works to provide jobs. By 1933, more than 1.5 million Canadians were on some form of public relief, and the official unemployment rate was 23 percent.

In 1935, at the height of the Depression, 2,000 desperate unemployed men (ABOVE) set out from Kamloops, British Columbia, in a great trek. The men were en route to Ottawa to demand a guaranteed minimum wage, but

their voices were never heard in the capital. Riots and the killing of a police detective halted their course in Saskatoon.

The devastating effects of the Depression were not felt by the Trudeau family. In 1933, they left for a summer in Europe aboard a luxury ocean liner (OPPOSITE). The voyage was made possible by the profits from the sale of their service stations a year earlier. While many Montrealers were facing eviction, the Trudeaus' prosperity allowed them to purchase a three-storey house in the heart of Outremont. Charles enjoyed his money, supporting local sports teams and athletes, and travelling extensively with his friends and family.

Trudeau in Transit

The Trudeau family's months in Europe during the summer of 1933 were a time of exploration and independence for the adolescent Pierre.

The Depression had also seized Europe, and the continent was witnessing the awakening of fascist political forces. In Germany, Pierre heard the revving of Nazi soldiers' motorcycles and in Italy he stood in the square and saw the balcony from which Benito Mussolini had mesmerized crowds of Roman citizens. The significance of these encounters made little impression on the young Trudeau. He enjoyed Venice's Piazza San Marco (OPPOSITE), unaware that boys not much older than he sat around radios listening to German Führer Adolf Hitler's call to arms (BELOW). The unleashing of Nazi forces (LEFT) in Europe was imminent.

Philosopher King

After his summer in Europe, Pierre returned to the classical Jesuit school Collège Jean-de-Brébeuf in Montreal. Encouraged by the teachings of the Jesuit brothers, he took to his studies with determined enthusiasm. When the curriculum alone did not fill his hunger for knowledge, he immersed himself in the works of Aristotle, Plato, and Jean Jacques Rousseau (ABOVE).

Anglo Mores

In the spring of 1935, Pierre's life changed radically. While in Florida at the Montreal Royals' training camp, his father suddenly contracted pneumonia and died before returning to Quebec. Grace Trudeau suddenly became the most influential force in her children's lives. Her traditional Anglo background and English mores became a dominant force in the Trudeau household. French was rarely spoken among the family members.

Pierre's summer months, which had previously been enjoyed at the family's home on Lac Tremblant, were now spent at Upper Canada's elite Camp Ahmek (LEFT). It was at Ahmek, located in Ontario's Algonquin Park, that Pierre nurtured his lifelong affection for nature and canoeing. Here, childhood stories of the adventures of the *coureurs de bois* (BELOW) suddenly sprang to life.

In 1937, Prime Minister William Lyon Mackenzie King (RIGHT) paid a visit to Berlin. Following his discussions with Hitler and other German leaders, King announced that he had succeeded in promoting "understanding, friendship, and goodwill" with the Führer. King would soon realize Hitler's catastrophic ambitions; the young Trudeau would remain uninterested in politics until late in World War II.

Faces of the Nation

On September 10, 1939, Canada declared war on Nazi Germany. As battles began in Europe, Pierre Trudeau (LEFT) graduated from Brébeuf College and in 1940 enrolled in the law program at the University of Montreal (BELOW).

While Trudeau studied and men went to war, Canadians were busy producing weapons (OPPOSITE, TOP LEFT), food, and supplies for its military forces. In 1942, when the Allied armies prepared to increase their initiatives in Africa, Europe, and Asia, the demand for soldiers once again came to the forefront of Canadian politics. Anti-conscription rallies were held frequently in Montreal (OPPOSITE, TOP MIDDLE). At one of them, Jean Drapeau, a young Montreal lawyer, thundered, "No to conscription – No to broken promises!" He was referring to a promise made by Mackenzie King in 1940 that conscription would not be invoked. Trudeau openly supported Drapeau. On April 27, 1942, a conscription referendum was held. Sixty-three percent of Canadians voted in favour of mandatory military service; in Quebec, nearly 73 percent voted against it.

English Canadians, who had already expressed their intolerance of minorities by detaining Japanese Canadians (OPPOSITE, TOP RIGHT), were unwilling to accept Quebec's indifference towards the war. By 1944, navy convoys, seen here (OPPOSITE, MIDDLE) passing through the St. Lawrence River, were carrying conscripts from every region of Canada, including Quebec. Finally, helped by the efforts of Allied forces like these Canadians in Ortona, Italy, in 1943 (OPPOSITE, BOTTOM LEFT), the landing of Allied forces on mainland Europe in 1944, and the detonation of two atomic bombs (OPPOSITE, BOTTOM RIGHT) over Japan in 1945, the war came to an end. The bitter divides between French and English Canadians, however, would linger long after the troops returned home.

The Individual and Society

In the autumn of 1944, following a year of articling at a downtown Montreal law firm, Trudeau experienced an awakening much greater than the one he attempted to impose on his friend Roger Rolland (OPPOSITE) in Paris. Encouraged by André Laurendeau, a popular Quebec nationalist, Trudeau spent the next four years studying political economy at the world's most prestigious institutions, including Harvard University, École libre des sciences politiques in Paris, and the London School of Economics. Experiences at each of these institutions built the foundation of Trudeau's philosophical beliefs and helped shape his political future.

The lessons learned outside the classroom during this period also proved to have a lasting effect on Trudeau. In an America brimming with life and optimism (BELOW LEFT), Trudeau realized for the first time that Quebec was becoming an increasingly secular society. While living in Paris (BELOW MIDDLE), he met the philosopher Emmanuel Mounier, whose teachings influenced Trudeau's thoughts on the individual and society. Finally, at the London School of Economics, where every political and cultural walk of life was found, he saw the beginnings of the welfare state led by England's Labour Party. Postwar London (BOTTOM RIGHT) was a hotbed of socialist and liberal ideals.

1948 | Onward East

Revolutionary Voyage

In the spring of 1948, Trudeau set out on a year-long journey that took him through Eastern Europe, Israel (BELOW LEFT), the Middle East, India (BELOW RIGHT), Indochina, China, and Hong Kong. His journey was initiated by the need to complete his yet-unfinished Harvard doctoral thesis on the interplay between the doctrines of Christianity and Marxism. Although Trudeau didn't finish his post-graduate degree, he saw this trip as a personal challenge and the culmination of the journey he began in 1944.

In China, Communist forces led by Mao Zedong faced the Nationalist forces of Chiang Kai-Shek. Only days before Mao's army took Shanghai, Trudeau was in the city to witness the Nationalist army in retreat. As Mao's army advanced on the city, supplies dwindled and Chiang Kai-Shek's desperate leaders executed suspected collaborators (OPPOSITE), leaving their bodies to rot in the hot sun.

Suddenly I seized the curved double-edged dagger one of them wore in his belt and pretended to examine it. They were outraged at this deception and started yelling more than ever. But I replied with phrases borrowed from every known language, and a few others besides, sometimes raising my voice, alternating between sweet talk and melancholy; I recited poetry, performed drama, started a speech. Each time I took a breath, they tried to put in a word edgewise, but I started up again, with still more sparkle in my eyes and more forceful gestures. This put-on of mine worked. The three louts feared madness more than any handgun, and beat an anxious retreat down the steps without letting me out of sight. I was ruthless. I was determined to witness the complete obliteration of their self-respect and I had all the force of a firebrand. They didn't dare look at the crazed and wildly gesticulating silhouette looming above them. They fled into the desert to escape my wrath, focusing their eyes straight ahead and, if I may say so, keeping their tail between their legs.

PIERRE ELLIOTT TRUDEAU | LETTER FROM MESOPOTAMIA | DECEMBER 2, 1949

Return Home

In 1949, Trudeau, along with hundreds of war refugees, returned to North America by ship. This young boy (OPPOSITE), a displaced child found in the rubble of Europe, disembarked in Halifax after a transatlantic voyage. His stoic face was just one of the millions the country would welcome in the coming decades. In the years following the war, new waves of immigration made Canada into an increasingly multicultural society, a reality slow to manifest itself in the political realm. In 1948, St. Laurent (LEFT, WEARING GLASSES), here being handed the reins of the Liberal Party by King, who had been its leader for almost thirty years, would take the country into the next decade. Following the chaos of World War II, the nation, like these residents of Chicoutimi, Quebec (BELOW), was ready to turn its gaze to the future and enjoy the luxuries of a peacetime era.

**Into Power
1949 to 1968**

Into Power | Alison Gordon

THE MAN WHO DEFINED POLITICAL LIFE for the postwar generation of Canadians is the proverbial riddle wrapped inside an enigma, and when it comes to Pierre Elliott Trudeau, you can take that tiny parcel of ambiguity, put it inside a conundrum, wrap a couple of lengths of contradiction around it, and tie it off neatly in a knot.

I am part of that postwar generation, born just a tick or two ahead of the boom, and the first time I was eligible to vote was in the 1968 election that began Trudeau's long era in power. I voted Liberal that day, for the only time in my life, truly believing that I was voting for dramatic change.

I wasn't the only one, of course, to put my political dreams in Pierre Trudeau's hands. I wasn't the only one, either, to see those dreams disappear into some dusty corner of the East Block. But on that golden June morning of my first vote, I thought that I was ending world hunger, banning the bomb, uniting English and French Canada, and, oh, probably legalizing marijuana while I was at it, with my proudly vehement X.

OF COURSE I WAS NAÏVE, BUT I CAN FORGIVE MYSELF FOR that under the circumstances. I had played a small part in the process that brought Trudeau to power and felt as if I had a personal stake in the vision.

The election campaign of 1968 had been like no other. The nightly newscasts had been filled with footage of screaming teens and their swooning mums, and the inevitable kisses. Trudeau brought a glamour to Canadian politics, against which decent, hard-working, old-style politicians like Robert Stanfield, his Conservative opponent, didn't stand a chance. After years of watching Mike Pearson, John Diefenbaker, and Tommy Douglas fight it out in the House, the electorate, particularly that big new young electorate, was ready to send The Grandpas to the showers and make room for this swinging bachelor with the flirty eyes and enigmatic smile.

The media called it "Trudeaumania." They got it wrong, of course, at least partly so. Support for Trudeau among many of the young voters was more than skin deep.

The generation that came of age in that era was a highly politicized one. The anti-Vietnam War movement was in full swing, as were free-speech movements on campuses across North America. We were an intense generation, bent on social change, and we believed that Trudeau represented our chance to make our voices heard.

I guess I was as good an example as any of my political generation. I was passionate about politics. I had sat down in front of a missile base in Northern Quebec in 1964, and marched on Washington a year later. I had been in Quebec City during the Queen's controversial state visit in 1964, where I watched the separatist leader Pierre Bourgault deliver a passionate oration at a street rally; I saw the Queen's cavalcade through streets lined, shoulder to shoulder, with members of the military, and was chased, terrified, through the narrow twisting streets of Old Quebec by truncheon-waving riot police.

I went back to university and studied French-Canadian politics. I learned about Duplessis and the Quiet Revolution, and gained

Darkness and Duplessis

Quebec Premier Maurice Duplessis, leader of the Union Nationale since 1936, unveils a statue of Father Marie-Victorin under the watchful eye of Cardinal Paul-Émile Léger. Duplessis's government, in alliance with the ultra-conservative Quebec Church, controlled every aspect of life in the province. Political and bureaucratic leaders were handpicked by the premier; the backgrounds of candidates applying for teaching posts were scrutinized to ensure that their beliefs did not contradict the mores of the government; social welfare was granted through Church-run hospitals and charities; and public education was synonymous with Catholic education.

Duplessis's time in power was known as the Great Darkness. This period in Quebec history was dominated by a political class that taught its citizens to respect their heritage and fear the influences of socialism and the Anglo world that threatened to destroy the province's social order. Upon his return to Canada in 1949, Pierre Trudeau – whose progressive foreign schooling branded him a radical – felt the Union Nationale's sting when he was denied a teaching position in the University of Montreal's faculty of law.

five day week
old age assistance
eight hour day
factory inspection
compulsory education
industrial standards
minimum wages
employment services

L'UNION
EST ICI
POUR DE BON

THE UNION
IS HERE
TO STAY

L'UNION
EST ICI
POUR DE BON

LABOR

some understanding of the roots of separatism. I also learned about the 1949 Asbestos Strike, and a young lawyer named Pierre Elliott Trudeau. I read *Cité libre* as well as I could with my rather rudimentary French, and came to admire Trudeau as a radical thinker with the courage to oppose the establishment. Later that year, when I got a chance to hear him speak at a conference, I jumped at it. I don't remember what he spoke about, I am afraid. I think it was something quite dry and academic. But I'll never forget the impression he made on me that afternoon.

He was smart, he was elegant, he was charming, and he was more. He seemed, even then, larger than his relatively modest size, and he filled the lecture hall with his presence. He had, as I was not the first to discover, charisma. He mesmerized me. He still does, no matter what I have thought of his politics from time to time.

A couple of years later, in the fall of 1967, I was living in Ottawa when the rumours began that Trudeau, then the justice minister in Mike Pearson's cabinet, was contemplating entering the race to replace Pearson as Liberal leader. On a whim, I tracked down the just-rented headquarters of his as-yet-unannounced campaign and told them I wanted to help. The place was in an office building, only partly furnished, with cardboard boxes all around and telephones sitting on the floor. I expected to be given envelopes to stuff – I was after all, a woman of the New Left, accustomed to back-room drudgery. Instead, my best friend from university, Jennifer Rae, and I were put in charge of publicity for the campaign.

It seems astounding to me now that a couple of 24-year-old women with virtually no experience in politics or communications would be handed that sort of responsibility, but that's the kind of campaign it was. Maybe it was because there was a sense of unreality about those early days. The campaign bosses were busy with the political stuff, someone had to handle the publicity, and there we were. By the time the campaign was up and running and we found ourselves in competition with every major ad agency in Canada, we'd already done most of the work.

We wrote the press kits, chose the photos, designed the posters and buttons, and generally created the look of the campaign. There were other young people working on the campaign, doing similar things in other areas, and we were taken seriously. All of our opinions were listened to in meetings. I think we were able to pull it off because no one thought to tell us we couldn't, and it made us quite giddy.

It also made us extraordinarily audacious: the central image of the campaign, the stark high-contrast poster of Trudeau so reminiscent of the Che Guevara poster that hung in hippie crash pads in that era, was judged by the political bosses to be too far out, and they vetoed it. Outraged, we did an end-run around them. Our pal Hal Kroeker, one of the young speechwriters, got a copy of the photo to Trudeau, who said he liked it. Swearing an oath of silence, we went ahead and ordered 5,000 posters and made sure they were available on the convention floor.

On the Friday night dedicated to the candidates' speeches, Jennifer and I got to the convention centre in time to hear Trudeau. I remember standing on one of the entrance ramps on the second level waiting for him to be announced. The other candidates had been surrounded by hullabaloo and had demonstrations preceding their addresses. We had been among

Rebel with a Cause

In the politically intolerant environment of Duplessis's Quebec, it did not take long before Trudeau (FAR LEFT) put his intellect and ideology into practice. During the spring of 1949, 5,000 members of the Canadian Catholic Confederation of Labour (CCCL) organized an illegal strike in Asbestos, Quebec. The miners, who extracted asbestos (TOP RIGHT), were protesting against poor working conditions and exploitative management practices. Gérard Pelletier, a close friend of Trudeau's, who was reporting on the protest for *Le Devoir*, invited the young lawyer to Asbestos only a few days after his return to Canada.

Trudeau spent only a short time with Pelletier in the Eastern Townships, but the trip became part of his legend. At the invitation of the strike's chief organizer, a firebrand named Jean Marchand, Trudeau addressed a rally. Marchand

had asked him to talk about the strikers' legal rights. Instead, the young man with the blond beard spoke passionately about their human rights and the importance of throwing off the yoke of their oppressors. Then he went home to Montreal. When the asbestos workers returned to the mine's changing rooms (MIDDLE RIGHT) after four months off the job, they had won no concessions, but they had transformed the Quebec labour climate, as the mural showing a poised "Labor" fist about to strike a hapless boss (BOTTOM FAR LEFT) suggests. In Trudeau's introduction to a book about the strike, he would call it "a turning point in the entire religious, political, social, and economic history of the Province of Quebec."

Before the Asbestos Strike, Quebec's Catholic trade unions had been conservative organizations that promoted cooperation over confrontation. After the strike, they grew more militant and less

tied to the Church. In 1960, the CCCL became the Confederation of National Trade Unions, leaving behind its religious affiliation entirely. Meanwhile, Quebecers took on greater roles in the country's central labour organizations. In 1954 Claude Jodoin (BOTTOM RIGHT) became national president of the Trades and Labor Congress of Canada, which merged with the Canadian Congress of Labour in 1956 to form the Canadian Labour Congress with Jodoin as its first president.

The Quebec union movement achieved a common front when the CCCL joined forces with the Quebec Federation of Labour during the bitter seven-month Murdochville Strike, which began in March 1957 (BOTTOM MIDDLE). The strike ended in failure, but the alliance between Catholic and secular unions was a sign of things to come.

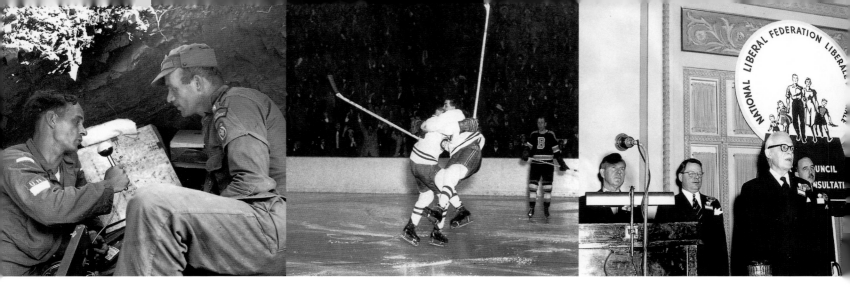

Fifties Faces

In June 1950, when the Communist forces of North Korea marched across the South Korean border, the United States army, led by General Douglas MacArthur, spearheaded an international contingent, which included Canadian forces, to defend South Korea. A young René Lévesque (ABOVE LEFT, HOLDING MICROPHONE) went to Korea to be a war correspondent.

In Canada, the frustration of French Canadians against the English establishment grew. After Maurice "Rocket" Richard (ABOVE CENTRE) was suspended just before the 1955 Stanley Cup finals for a vicious attack on a Boston opponent, Montreal fans took to the streets to protest. Many Québécois saw the suspension as a ploy by the National Hockey League's English president, Clarence Campbell, to put *les Canadiens* at a disadvantage against their Anglo counterparts. Trudeau, who worked for the Privy Council in Ottawa from 1949 until 1951, was also inflamed over the plight of French Canadians in the English-dominated capital. After leaving Ottawa he noted that the French there were viewed as "trained donkeys" by the country's ruling Anglos.

those who had argued vigorously, and finally successfully, that Trudeau should make his entrance without fanfare and dancing girls, and we were terrified that we had been wrong.

Finally his name was called. He walked through the crowds alone in the spotlight as hundreds of black and white placards – our posters – appeared all over the hall, especially in the level where the general public sat. It was electrifying.

"Let's see them claim that was spontaneous," cracked a reporter standing near us, unaware of who we were. Jennifer and I went back to the office. There was still a lot of work to be done.

LOOKING BACK MORE THAN 30 YEARS LATER, IT IS hard to recapture the mood of that time, so much has changed. In the 60s, our literature, theatre, film, and music were dominated by British and American creators and performers. We were a country whose identity was still evolving. And then came 1967, our centennial year, and a celebration that surprised Canadians as much as it surprised the rest of the world. Throwing off our dour reserve, we sang songs and held festivals and built concert halls and travelled from one end of the country to another, discovering along the way how much we had in common. Of course, that year all roads led to Montreal and the site of Expo '67.

It was a world's fair like no other, with a theme nothing less than Man and His World. The pavilions were like something out of Futurama fantasies, with each country scrambling to outdo the next in imagination and daring. There was theatre from around the world and multi-screen movies with cutting-edge technology. It was the place to be that year, and the city was packed to the rafters with tourists who fell under its sophisticated cosmopolitan spell.

In memory, the sun always shone on that Montreal summer, or there was a full moon in a clear sky over the St. Lawrence River. It was a shiny time, full of laughter and balloons and music in the air. It was a summer of chance encounters and bold adventures. For that one glorious season, being Canadian wasn't dull and stodgy. Suddenly (and briefly) we were sexy. It was the country's fifteen minutes in the spotlight, and we basked in its unaccustomed glow.

And those of us who were there, particularly those of us who were old enough to be there on our own and young enough to enjoy it – those of us, in other words, in that postwar boom – had our expectations, if not our lives, changed by the experience.

And six months later, the Liberal Party chose a new leader.

Coincidence? I don't think so. The man suited the mood of the times.

The leadership convention was held on the first weekend in April 1968. In the closing days of the campaign, Jennifer and I ordered a new bunch of buttons. They had no candidate affiliation on them at all, except that they happened to use the same font and orange colour as the rest of the Trudeau material. The message was simple: "It's spring!"

We were doing more than just responding to the Robert Winters leadership slogan ("It's Winters Time"). We were tapping into the national mood. Canadian spring is a time of hope and daring, a

Prime Minister Louis St. Laurent (OPPOSITE RIGHT) was content to focus his attention on the country's growing economy rather than its linguistic divide. His top bureaucrats, holdovers from Mackenzie King's twenty-one years in office, were guiding the country through a time of robust expansion supported primarily by the export of Canadian resources to the United States and by the establishment of American branch plants on Canadian soil. The St. Lawrence Power Project (ABOVE LEFT), completed in 1958, was a precursor to the St. Lawrence Seaway, an engineering feat that linked industrial objectives of both countries. In 1953, Trudeau warned Canadians that "in key sectors of the Canadian economy, non-residents are in a position to take decisions quite foreign to the welfare of Canadians." For the moment, such pleas had little effect on most Canadians, who, like these women at a Montreal diner (ABOVE RIGHT), were busy enjoying the affluence of the postwar era and the rewards of cosmopolitan life.

time for falling in love and for planting seeds, for leaps of blind faith. We thought it was a pretty good metaphor for our campaign.

I've still got one of those buttons pinned to a bookcase in my study, one of the few relics I kept from that campaign; that and a photo of Jennifer and me just after it was all over, two young women, exhausted, crying tears of triumphant joy. We were never more beautiful in our lives.

I look back on those days with some embarrassment now. My political naïveté is stunning in hindsight. Like others of my generation, I completely misjudged the complexity of Trudeau's relationship with Quebec, for one thing. I was disillusioned by the imposition of the War Measures Act just a few years later. I expected far too much of Trudeau, and he couldn't help but let me down. I never voted Liberal again.

But I wouldn't have missed that moment in Ottawa for anything.

I STILL FIND PIERRE TRUDEAU FASCINATING, AND I'VE never come close to figuring him out. Almost 25 years after the campaign during which we first met, I found myself back at the Ottawa Civic Centre with him. We had been filmed reminiscing about those days, and we went to look for some lunch. The Central Canada Exhibition was about to open, and the grounds were full of frantic preparations. As we walked towards the food tent, the workers began to notice him in their midst. They waved and smiled and called out his name. They were English Canadians and French Canadians and recent immigrants, seedy carny barkers and big guys in work boots and little grandmothers at the food stands and blushing teenagers (still!); they all greeted him as if he were an old friend. Trudeau smiled and shook hands with them all, but not like other politicians I've seen. He wasn't feeding off their adulation. Neither did he seem irritated by the attention. He just acknowledged it, but was otherwise unaffected by it.

The scene illustrated the kind of contradiction that somehow defines the man: here is a guy famous for his love of privacy who felt no apparent need to escape the attention of strangers; an aloof intellectual millionaire happy to hob nob for a few minutes with the common folk.

Early in his political life, Trudeau was asked how badly he wanted to be prime minister. "Not badly at all," he said at the time, quoting Plato to the effect that people who wanted power badly were the wrong people to give it to. It was a disingenuous response, perhaps, but the voters of Canada bought it, over and over again. The man who was our most unlikely politician went on to become the longest-serving elected head of his government. And no matter what he did at home, he never embarrassed us abroad, which is more than you can say for any prime minister since.

I have encountered him a number of times in the past 30-odd years. Our paths have crossed at parties, on the campaign trail, at book events, formal dinners, casual luncheons, even at a few baseball games. He always greets me with the same air of warm amusement, as if he and I share some sort of secret. Problem is, I've never figured out what the secret is. And I probably never will.

Meeting of Minds

"Social reformer, poet, and activist" was how Trudeau (OPPOSITE) characterized F.R. Scott (BELOW), his early mentor, at the former McGill University dean of law's seventieth birthday celebrations in 1969. The friendship of Scott and Trudeau was steeped in their love of nature, freedom, and intellectual challenge. In the summer of 1956, following the publication of *The Asbestos Strike*, a project Scott and Trudeau had collaborated on since 1954, the two men embarked in a plane (CENTRE, TOP) and set out on a journey to the Mackenzie River (CENTRE, MIDDLE AND BOTTOM), a trip that Scott photographed extensively. Scott's key influences on Trudeau included his emphasis on the need for a strong constitution in a democracy, his views on capitalism's failings, and his belief in a just society where every individual has an equal opportunity to achieve success. Following their wilderness exploration, Scott described Trudeau in one of his poems as "A man testing his strength, Against the strength of his country."

1957 | Non-Partisan Politician

King of Mount Royal

Courted to join both the Quebec Liberal Party and the federal Co-operative Commonwealth Confederation (CCF) during the latter part of the 1950s, Trudeau involved himself in non-partisan organizations only. The future prime minister's reluctance to join political life, however, did not mean that he was out of the public eye. His strong critiques of the Duplessis government published in *Cité libre* (RIGHT), a political magazine founded in 1950 by Trudeau and five others, granted him the respect of many of Quebec's most prominent social leaders, including the union chief Gérard Picard, seen here (BELOW) talking to Trudeau on Montreal's Mount Royal in 1957, and André Laurendeau, one of the province's esteemed intellectuals. After the 1956 publication of *The Asbestos Strike*, a book that attacked Duplessis's reactionary brand of Quebec nationalism, Laurendeau stated in *Le Devoir*, "The best part of Trudeau, besides his technical competence, is his love of liberty: he is prepared to run its risks as well as claim its advantages. A remarkable personality has been revealed."

Chief Dief

In June 1957, when the country granted John Diefenbaker's Conservatives a minority government, Louis St. Laurent (LEFT, IN CENTRE) and the federal Liberal Party were forced to leave office after twenty-two years of rule in Canada. After a mere eight months in power, Prime Minister Diefenbaker and his newly sworn-in cabinet (BELOW) found themselves fighting another election campaign. Confident that they could win a majority government, the Conservatives had engineered their own defeat in a parliamentary vote of non-confidence in order to initiate an election. The Liberals, now facing the electorate with the Nobel-prize-winner Lester B. Pearson at their helm, proved to be no match for Dief's Tories, who were swept into office with the largest majority to date.

The Conservatives' mandate, however, was plagued with indecision from the outset. Bowing to White House pressure, Diefenbaker cancelled the production of Canada's Avro Arrow fighter-bomber in favour of American Bomarc missiles. Trudeau used *Cité libre* to voice frustrations that many Canadians felt about their government, "Mr. Diefenbaker's good intentions have flopped so often," wrote Trudeau, "that flops are without a doubt the leading characteristics of his style."

古壁省自由党政治提綱

宣言：

（一）関於教育建設問題：

1. 凡自由党得選，本省中小
学、大学，所有学校全部免費。

2. 全部書籍由学校供給免費
使用。

3. 青年児童一律在基本上可享
受由通齡達至十六歲的文化教
育。

4. 建立省立大学服務處。

5. 建立特別服務處幫助學生財
政問題。

6. 建立現代化技術学校，為發展
本省之工業。

（二）関於社會福利問題：

1. 凡若自由党得選，對於児童救
助費，由十六歲十八歲的就学救
助童仍得享受每月拾元的幫助。

2. 凡若自由党得選，養老費提及
在原有的月費增加拾元，即現
拾伍元可得陸拾伍元。

（武）関於這個問題有下列回点：

1. 七十歲以上及超過七十歲以上的老
経領得養老金。

2. 六十五歲至七十歲以上已獲得預
拾伍元以上有欠点者，已領得補助
金。

3. 健康上有欠点者，已領得補助
金。

4. 盲目者已領得補助金。

Without a Cause

The political landscape of Quebec changed dramatically on September 7, 1959, when Maurice Duplessis died suddenly after suffering a series of strokes. The following year, the Quebec Liberal Party, under the leadership of Jean Lesage, narrowly defeated the Union Nationale, ushering in a period of modernization and growth that would become known as the Quiet Revolution. The face of Quebec society, like that of the rest of Canada, was changing. The Lesage campaign poster (FAR LEFT), expressing the politician's message in Chinese characters, reveals the increasingly multi-ethnic makeup of the country.

After the Lesage victory, Quebec's anti-Duplessis reformers, who had fought so hard during the 1950s, suddenly found themselves in positions of power. For Trudeau, the death of Duplessis and the ensuing defeat of the Union Nationale meant that he was finally granted a professorship at the University of Montreal's faculty of law. Despite this long-sought-after victory, Trudeau suddenly found himself without a cause. Those close to him recognized his restless spirit and cited his frequent travels as evidence of unsettled ambitions. In fall 1960, Trudeau and his close friend Jacques Hébert (ABOVE, TRUDEAU AT LEFT), a Montreal publisher and writer, journeyed to China for several weeks with a delegation of French Canadians who had been invited to see the October parades in Tiananmen Square in Beijing and sights including the Great Wall (TOP RIGHT). Following their trip, Hébert and Trudeau wrote a short book about their experiences entitled *Deux Innocents en Chine rouge* (*Two Innocents in Red China*).

Hello, Mr. President

In May 1961, Canadians eagerly welcomed the striking American first couple, President John F. Kennedy and his glamorous wife, Jacqueline, to Ottawa. Seen here (OPPOSITE) being greeted by John Diefenbaker and his wife, Olive, the sophisticated Kennedys offered a noticeable contrast to their ardently traditional Canadian counterparts. Seven years after the Kennedys' visit, Canadians would be mesmerized by another charismatic leader, Pierre Trudeau. Following Trudeau's 1968 appeal to voters, "Come take my hand and we will adventure together," *Time* magazine described Trudeau's speeches as "reminiscent of John Kennedy."

Montreal in the early 1960s was enjoying an exciting new era. Dorval Airport opened outside the city, seen here (BELOW LEFT) in contrast to a nun wearing a traditional habit. At the start of a new decade, Canadians were getting ready to push the limits, test the rules, and question traditions. The jazzy tunes and hip lifestyles of the Beatniks (BELOW RIGHT) opened the door to a floodgate of changes, which would be marked in large part by Trudeau's entry into politics.

Economic reform is impossible so long as legislators, lawyers, and business men cling to economic concepts which were conceived for another age. The liberal idea of property helped to emancipate the bourgeoisie but it is now hampering the march towards economic democracy. The ancient values of private property have been carried over into the age of corporate wealth. As a result, our laws and our thinking recognize as proprietors of an enterprise men who today hold a few shares which they will sell tomorrow on the stock market; whereas workers who may have invested the better part of their lives and of their hopes in a job have no proprietary right to that job, and may be expropriated from it without compensation whenever a strike or lock-out occurs, whenever they grow old, or whenever Capital decides to disinvest.

PIERRE ELLIOTT TRUDEAU | MCGILL LAW JOURNAL | FEBRUARY 1962

Maîtres and Militants

The popular broadcaster René Lévesque (OPPOSITE), seen here in the studios of Radio Canada, joined Jean Lesage's Liberal Party in 1960. Well known and respected throughout Quebec for his engaging journalistic style, Lévesque soon gained political prominence as the province's minister of natural resources. In 1962, Lévesque convinced Lesage to hold a provincial election in which the primary issue was the deprivatization of Quebec's hydroelectric industry, which, like so many other industries in Quebec, was almost completely operated by Anglo society. The campaign slogan, *Maîtres Chez Nous* (Masters in Our Own House), was a clear indication of the party's intention to gain control of their province.

During the next four years of the Liberal Party's mandate, Lesage and Lévesque sometimes clashed over the question of how much autonomy Quebec needed from the rest of Canada. Lévesque became increasingly separatist in his thinking. In 1964 he stated, "Either Quebec will become an associate state within Canada, with a status guaranteeing it the economic, political and cultural powers necessary for its growth as a nation, or else Quebec will become independent, free to choose its own destiny." These words were uttered in a climate of increasing unrest, most dramatically illustrated by the series of bombings engineered by the revolutionary Front de libération du Québec (FLQ).

During the second six months of 1964, nationalist Quebecers could watch with amusement as the rest of Canada engaged in a passionate debate over a new flag. Traditionalists, often of British heritage, were determined to hang on to the Red Ensign, with its Union Jack firmly ensconced in the upper left-hand corner. Progressives, many of whom joined the demonstrators on Parliament Hill (ABOVE), favoured the prime minister's proposed design, the so-called Pearson Pennant, with its three red maple leaves as the central symbol. The winning design, with its single red maple leaf, pleased almost no one.

Reluctant Bride

In 1965, Prime Minister Pearson announced the fifth federal election in only eight years. For the majority of Canadians, it was not clear why the government felt it necessary to pursue public consent: the economy was still riding the postwar boom; the Maple Leaf was accepted as the nation's flag; and Canada's status as a nuclear nation, a policy heavily debated in the 1963 election, was under less protest. In spite of the turbulent anti-Pearson emotions expressed by these western protesters (ABOVE), it was ultimately a politician's election, intended to elect one of the federal parties with a clear majority, thereby ending a string of minority governments.

Pierre Elliott Trudeau entered federal politics as a reluctant bride. In early September 1965, he announced his candidacy for the Liberal Party (OPPOSITE) along with his close allies Jean Marchand (SEATED, SMOKING A PIPE), a highly respected Quebec union leader, and Gérard Pelletier, the influential editor of *La Presse*. Collectively, the group was known as "the three wise men." It was the Liberal Party's hope that Marchand, its plum candidate, would establish strong ties between Ottawa and Quebec. Pelletier and Trudeau were permitted to run as candidates only after Marchand used his considerable negotiating skills to convince the Liberal Party of their loyalty. On November 8, 1965, the three wise men were elected to Parliament.

1967 | Expo 67

Justice Minister

In spring 1967, as Canadians began Centennial celebrations (RIGHT), Trudeau was sworn into Pearson's cabinet as justice minister, along with other first-time ministers Jean Chrétien and John Turner (BELOW). Until 1967, Trudeau had barely been seen in Ottawa. Selected by Pearson to take on the role of prime minister's parliamentary secretary in 1966, he had spent the majority of his time learning valuable diplomatic skills while representing Canadian interests in France, Franco-African countries, and at the United Nations.

As justice minister, Trudeau wasted little time before he introduced controversial reforms. His Omnibus Bill, presented to the House of Commons in December 1967, was intended to modernize Canada's antiquated Criminal Code. Trudeau's proposed legislation made it easier for women to be granted a divorce; it decriminalized homosexuality; and it reduced the restrictions on access to abortion. Faced by a barrage of Conservative arguments, Trudeau responded, "The state has no business in the bedrooms of the nation." A devout Roman Catholic, the justice minister demonstrated his eagerness to take on difficult issues with determination and poise.

The timing of the Omnibus Bill could not have been better for Trudeau. Prior to its release, he was still widely unknown to Canadians outside Quebec. However, by the time Prime Minister Pearson announced his resignation in December, Trudeau's face and words were well known across the country. After Jean Marchand – the man many felt would be Pearson's obvious replacement – declined his candidacy for the leadership, the field for a successor was suddenly wide open. Trudeau, however, kept hidden any desire to become party leader. Before the justice minister departed for a holiday to Tahiti in late December, a reporter asked him to comment on the rumour that he might run in the Liberal leadership campaign. To this, Trudeau responded, "Are you serious?"

Vive le Québec libre

While Pierre Trudeau spent his summer in Ottawa tirelessly working on his controversial Omnibus Bill, the world came to Canada's doorstep at Expo 67. "The cannonade of fireworks which marked the opening of Expo, bursting in a technicolour tattoo over the St. Lawrence on an April afternoon, may in retrospect turn out to have been one of those rare moments that change the direction of a nation's history," wrote Peter C. Newman on the day after Expo's official opening.

The two islands in the St. Lawrence, supporting an eclectic mix of futuristic architectural styles (LEFT), gave the nation a touch of class that earned it unprecedented world attention. But not all omens were optimistic during that buoyant centennial year. In July, when French President Charles de Gaulle visited Expo and declared from a Montreal balcony, *"Vive le Québec libre!"* he reminded everyone of the threat of separatism. In September, when a Montreal gang attacked a centennial event and an ugly fight with the RCMP ensued (BELOW), the issue once again came distressingly to the fore. In December, when the Royal Commission on Bilingualism and Biculturalism released the first volume of its report, Canadians were forced to face up to the serious linguistic inequities encountered by French Canadians.

Jockeying for Position

On April 6, 1968, the Ottawa Civic Centre (OPPOSITE) was awash in Liberal faces, colours, and political dreams. As the 2,396 Liberal delegates descended on Ottawa to select Prime Minister Pearson's successor, all eyes were on Trudeau.

In the months leading up to the convention, Trudeau's charmed campaign took on an astounding momentum. In January, Pearson had ordered the leadership hopefuls to stay in Ottawa and tend to their ministerial portfolios. However, Trudeau, who did not announce his candidacy until February 16, 1968, was allowed to travel across the country in preparation for a constitutional conference in the early part of the month. At the conference, Trudeau and Quebec Premier Daniel Johnson openly locked horns on national television over Trudeau's proposed Charter of Rights. Meticulously, Trudeau picked apart Johnson's arguments. In the lead-up to

the April leadership convention, Pierre Trudeau had won a crucial battle. Going into the convention weekend, a Gallup poll indicated that Trudeau's public support stood at 32 percent, a full 18 percentage points more than his closest rival, Paul Martin.

Confidence in Trudeau's ability to lead the Liberal Party was further bolstered on April 4, when Finance Minister Mitchell Sharp withdrew his candidacy in order to lend his considerable support to Trudeau. After months of speculation, speeches, hand-shaking, and deal-making, the Liberal leadership campaign came down to seven men and four ballots.

After an early ballot (ABOVE), Trudeau glanced back to Treasury Board president Edgar Benson (WITH PIPE), while Jean Marchand and Mitchell Sharp (TO TRUDEAU'S RIGHT) checked their notes.

61

The Party's Choice

With a charismatic grin and humble wave, Pierre Trudeau graciously acknowledges the cheers of his supporters (BELOW). As shown on the opposite page, Trudeau's opponents presented themselves in a variety of different ways. Paul Hellyer's campaign (TOP ROW LEFT) brought out the band and various letters of the alphabet to make its case. Following a disappointing third-ballot result, Hellyer indicated his withdrawal from the leadership race by promptly hoisting a Robert Winters placard high above his head and chanting, "Go, Bob, Go!" Trudeau, meanwhile, allowed his mastery of the written word (TOP ROW, RIGHT) to speak volumes to the masses. The key for Eric Kierans (MIDDLE ROW, LEFT) was to draw on the youth and fashion of the day. Kierans, who provided much of the campaign's intellectual thrust, fell short of his leadership aspirations after only the first round of voting. The use of puns by Winters (MIDDLE ROW, CENTRE) may have been catchy, but it was not enough to catch the high-flying Trudeau. Finishing second to Trudeau on the final ballot, Winters would be the only one of the candidates to retire from politics following his defeat. Paul Martin (MIDDLE ROW, RIGHT), seen by many as yesterday's man, pinned his hopes on his distinguished political record and extensive connections with the party's elite. After his disappointing first-ballot departure from the leadership race, Martin scribbled a brief withdrawal statement, "I have been caught in the generation gap." John Turner (BOTTOM ROW, LEFT, IN CENTRE OF PHOTO) entered the race with little hope of winning but as an opportunity to make his voice heard. In the end, it took four hard-fought ballots before the Liberal Party chose its successor to Lester B. Pearson. Their choice – Pierre Elliott Trudeau (BOTTOM ROW, RIGHT).

Watch Me
1968 to 1974

Watch Me | Peter Gzowski

MY ADMIRATION FOR PIERRE TRUDEAU was well developed long before 1968, when he assumed the leadership of the party he had so unexpectedly chosen; in the six years that followed, that admiration was to undergo much metamorphosis.

I had met him in Montreal, in 1961, where he was teaching law, writing for and helping to edit the influential journal *Cité libre*. I was working as the Quebec editor of *Maclean's*, struggling, with my inadequate French, to capture some of the people and events making the profound changes that were coursing through the province. I used the words "Quiet Revolution" so many times in my dispatches that many people thought, with flattering inaccuracy, that I'd coined the term. (In fact, the first use I've ever been able to track down, was, surprisingly enough, in the old Tory Toronto *Telegram*.) Though I hadn't yet met him, Trudeau's name kept cropping up in my research. He, or his writings, were in evidence in subjects as diverse as Paul-Émile Cardinal Léger, who turned out to be a closet supporter of *Cité libre*, and Jacques Hébert, whose publishing company, Les Éditions de l'homme, was carrying on its own fight against Duplessism. I decided to seek Trudeau out to see if he'd sit still for a *Maclean's* profile.

He was a reluctant subject, even then no fan of journalists or journalism. If he had any desire for the limelight, it was certainly not apparent to me. I persevered, pulling every string I could think of, Jacques Hébert, Gérard Pelletier, then the editor of *La Presse* and perhaps Trudeau's closest friend, and anyone else I'd met who might know him.

He eventually succumbed and one morning that spring I found myself ringing the bell at his mother's stately home in Outremont. He answered the door himself, and ushered me into the living room, dominated, as I remember, by a large, somewhat forbidding, European painting – Braque would have been my guess, but I was too intimidated to offer it.

"Like a drink?" he said.

Wow, I thought as I accepted, these Montreal intellectuals, into the sauce at 10 in the morning. Quel panache.

He brought me about four fingers of Scotch, neat, but, to my dismay, took nothing himself. Ah well, I thought, and proceeded to sip myself into a blissful fog, as we rambled through the first of what was to become the most challenging, stimulating and, in its own way, enjoyable series of conversations – nearly all of the later ones taking place, of course, on the radio – I have ever been lucky enough to be part of.

Interviewing him wasn't then – nor has it ever been – easy. He was as he has remained, as private as the Sphinx, apparently incapable of small talk, intolerant of pretense or stupidity, certain of his own opinions. But his mind was as penetrating as an épée and his erudition as formidable as a broadsword. He seemed to relish being challenged, provided you had thought your way through your question, and to delight in the Jesuitical adroitness of his response. As someone once said of Bobby Orr at his peak in the NHL, "he should play in a higher league."

My unabashedly admiring portrait of him ran in *Maclean's* under the title "Portrait of an Intellectual Engagé." It wasn't bad, I suppose, including, as it did, a prescient suggestion that if he ever entered politics he would be a force to be reckoned with, but

Into Office

It did not take long for Prime Minister Trudeau to steal the spotlight from Lester B. Pearson after being elected as Liberal Party leader and prime minister of Canada. Prior to the official handover of power, the two men met at 24 Sussex Drive (TOP) to discuss the formalities of their new roles. Bewitched by Trudeau since his presentation of the Omnibus Bill in December 1967, the media continued to treat him as an iconic figure. Countless images of the new prime minister being chased by young women on Parliament Hill (MIDDLE) flooded the papers as he provided Canadian politics with a sense of youthfulness and fun.

Out of the spotlight, Trudeau was aware that not everyone was enraptured by his ascent to stardom. "The fact that you have won means that others have lost," Trudeau reminded himself during his first days behind the prime minister's desk (BOTTOM). Many long-time Liberal Party members felt that the newcomer and his Quebec allies, chief among them Jean Marchand, Gérard Pelletier, and Marc Lalonde, had stolen the party from them. A decade after Trudeau became leader, Marchand stated in reference to the way he, Pelletier, and Trudeau had come to power, "We weren't Liberals but we decided to use the Liberal Party."

I never did hear whether he liked it or even, come to think of it, whether or not he read it.

GIVEN MY EARLIER ENCOUNTERS WITH TRUDEAU, IT was hard for me not to share in the excitement of his remarkable rise to victory: political unknown to MP, to parliamentary secretary, to justice minister in two years. And then, in 1968, Trudeaumania; he was elected prime minister, and would lead the country with a majority government.

To those of us who had been swept up in the American promise of John F. Kennedy and still mourned his death, Trudeau was especially inspiring. He was glamorous, he was sexy, and he was ours – the perfect symbol of the newly invigorated Canada that had emerged from Expo and the centennial celebrations.

From the outset, it was clear that high among Prime Minister Trudeau's priorities was a diffusion of the forces of Quebec nationalism. Quickly, any suspicions that his role in the intellectual circles of Montreal had aligned him with the separatist course so many of his friends and colleagues were now pursuing were erased, though no one who had read his work in *Cité libre* could ever have harboured such thoughts. Instead, Trudeau sought to strengthen Quebec's role in Confederation, to accelerate the progress reflected and supported by Lester Pearson's sweeping "Bi and Bi" commission, and to bring about a truly bilingual country. Among the first major pieces of legislation the new government brought in was the Official Languages Act, which entrenched bilingualism, as it said, "where numbers warrant." Trudeau was determined to attract some of the brightest young Québécois to Ottawa, as he himself had come in to work, however

On April 23, 1968, after several efforts were made to reconcile differences with the former leadership hopefuls, Trudeau announced a federal election for June 25. The prime minister wanted to go to the polls to capitalize on the momentum of the leadership campaign, rather than risk the assaults his minority government might face in the House of Commons if it completed the remaining two years of its current mandate. Some said that Trudeau's suave exterior concealed a certain ruthlessness. His decision to call a snap election denied outgoing Prime Minister Pearson his cherished chance to bid farewell to the House of Commons.

briefly, with the Privy Council nearly twenty years earlier.

In Quebec itself, however, the forces loosed by the Quiet Revolution continued to swirl. Everything was changing: the authority of the Church, the traditional role of women, the education system, the power of unions – virtually every facet of daily life. "Maîtres chez nous," the slogan of Jean Lesage's Liberal government, was taking on new meaning. Separatism, whose popularity had stood at just 13 percent in my days with *Maclean's*, grew steadily stronger, measuring now closer to 20 percent. Not long after Trudeau's ascent to power in Ottawa, René Lévesque, one of the principal architects of change and one of the most popular politicians in the province, stepped down from the Lesage cabinet to work with the movement that would soon become the Parti Québécois.

And then came October 1970. For some time, there'd been evidence of a group that called itself the Front de libération du Québec that was willing to work outside the law for the separatist cause – most seriously by planting bombs in the mailboxes of English Montreal. But, with the kidnapping of the British trade commissioner, James Cross, on October 5, high drama began to unfold. The rebels' demands included the release of the few of their members who were in jail, the reading of their "manifesto" on Radio-Canada, and safe passage out of the country for the kidnappers. Just as the Quebec government seemed ready to accede to at least some of the conditions – the manifesto had already been read – another hostage was abducted: Pierre Laporte, a minister of the Quebec government. Quebec asked for help from Ottawa, and,

on October 16, 1970, the Trudeau government, citing an "apprehended insurrection," brought in the War Measures Act, suspending many liberties and giving the authorities, among other powers, the right to haul people off to jail without charge.

This was a Pierre Trudeau we had not seen before; as ruthless in the suppression of civil rights as he had been steadfast in his defenses of them. In the broadest terms, his decisiveness did nothing to hurt his popularity. The War Measures Act passed the Commons with near unanimity, and the first surveys of public opinion found an astonishing 83 percent support – reinforced, no doubt, by the discovery of the body of Pierre Laporte, strangled and stuffed in a car trunk, the day after the Act came down.

Still, there were those who were troubled, not only by the sight of armed troops on the streets of Montreal, but by the draconian measures the prime minister had taken. In spite of my earlier infatuation with Trudeau, I was among them. I'd moved back to Toronto by this time, and was working at CBC Radio, where the powers of the government to limit free discussion of the Act or its consequences were keenly felt. Also, as the list of people who'd been rounded up in the middle of the night and held without bail or recourse to lawyers grew longer (it would total 450 names before the crisis was over), it included far too many people whose arrests seemed simply too bizarre to accept: the chanteuse Pauline Julien, the poet and later PQ cabinet minster Gérald Godin, the writer and bon-vivant Nick Auf der Maur, among others. I don't know if I thought of it then, but I have since wondered what would have happened if, instead of the gruesome murder of Pierre

Go Go Trudeau

Pierre Trudeau's political ascent coincided with one of the most notable years of the twentieth century. The historian Eric Hobsbawm described 1968 as "an age of flamboyant contradictions, of mindless hedonism and ideological revolt, of resolute optimism and of trips to hell." As countless protesters, including this one being dragged from Parliament (TOP ROW, LEFT), demonstrated for change, it became apparent that the status quo would no longer hold. Change had been predicted by Canada's mass-media guru, Marshall McLuhan (TOP ROW, MIDDLE), who had said a year earlier, "The medium is the message," a prediction that the world was entering an age in which politics would be driven by style over substance, form over content. McLuhan wrote to Trudeau after viewing him on television, "Your own image is a corporate mask, inclusive, requiring no private nuance whatever. This is your cool TV power. Iconic, sculptural." Trudeau's image, as described by McLuhan, captivated Canadians,

in particular its youth, its women, and its growing hippie counterculture (TOP ROW, RIGHT).

"Without Expo," wrote Richard Gwyn, "Trudeau could never have become Prime Minister." Trudeau took the youthful ideals of Expo and offered Canadians "a great adventure of discovery." Canadians, for their part, ate it up, as demonstrated by frenzied Trudeau supporters in Toronto (SECOND ROW, LEFT), Montreal (SECOND ROW, MIDDLE), and Victoria (SECOND ROW, RIGHT).

In stark opposition to the effervescent federal election campaign and the excitement of Trudeaumania were sobering international issues. While citizens of Czechoslovakia (THIRD ROW, LEFT) took to the streets against an onslaught of 650,000 Soviet troops determined to crush the modest democratic reforms enacted during the Prague Spring, Trudeau spoke of a Participatory Democracy that would allow all Canadians a greater voice in government. In the United States, the racial riots sparked by the assassination of Martin Luther King (THIRD ROW,

MIDDLE), on April 4, were far removed from the prime minister's vision of a Just Society, in which all citizens would be given equal opportunity to succeed. As Trudeau discussed government's need to protect the weak, the war in Vietnam (THIRD ROW, RIGHT) was reaching its zenith.

In the final days of the federal election campaign between Trudeau, NDP Leader Tommy Douglas, and Conservative Robert Stanfield, there was no doubt which Canadian political leader would be elected prime minister. While Radio-Canada's puppets (FOURTH ROW, LEFT) gave equal weight to each of their features, McLuhan read Trudeau's image best when he described his face as "the perfect mask – a charismatic mask. He has the face of a North American Indian." Trudeau was chief, the Canadian population his tribe, and the media his smoke signal. As cameras flashed, Trudeau literally dived (FOURTH ROW, MIDDLE) into Canadian political and pop culture, inspiring a band called the Sinners to release an album entitled *Go Go Trudeau* (FOURTH ROW, RIGHT).

Laporte, the handful of people who turned out to be behind the "apprehended insurrection" had just released their hostages in their underwear and let them run down Ste.-Catherine Street. They might have demonstrated how out of proportion to the real threat to peace the government's – and Trudeau's – reaction had been, and thereby served their cause more effectively. But the murder destroyed any chance for that.

In the fall of 1974, I had a chance to raise the matter of the War Measures Act with Trudeau. I suggested to him that if the Act had been brought down in the years when I first wrote about him, he, too, might have been among those rounded up in the midnight raids.

"Perhaps you're right," he said, "I had Karl Marx in my library and perhaps I would have been arrested and gone to jail. [But] I don't think I would have bitched about it. I would have bitched against the guys who created the climate in which the state, the elected representatives of the people, in order to defend the authority of the state, had to use strong measures."

He never did lose an argument.

That conversation, which took place in a radio studio in Toronto, was the last time I saw him in person until well after the next election. Much was to happen to him in the years that followed. In 1971, he married Margaret Sinclair (and broke a million hearts). In 1972, he fought the ineffectual "The Land Is Strong" election campaign that resulted in a Liberal minority government and taught Trudeau the political realities of trying to stay in power. He also continued his world travels, though as statesman now, not as the vagabond of his youth. The magic of Trudeaumania was ebbing, but he was still playing in a league of his own.

Occasionally, we saw the aloofness and contempt in which he held what he perceived to be wilful ignorance or simple stupidity. "Mange lo merge," he told grain farmers, "fuddle-duddle" (or something similar) he said in the House of Commons. "Just watch me," he crowed to a reporter who questioned his actions in the October Crisis.

I think now, looking back at those years, that he got a few things wrong. He never did come to understand the West, and there are still people in Alberta who have not forgiven him for his National Energy Policy. Curiously, for he knew Quebec and its principal players so well, his course of action to thwart the growth of separatism may have missed a seminal point: it was not a bilingual Canada the sovereigntists were after; it was a unilingual Quebec.

But there never was anyone like him, was there? And perhaps there never will be again.

I CONTINUED TO SEE HIM OCCASIONALLY OVER THE DECADES that followed. Once, in the 90s, in his law offices in Montreal, I had a few moments away from the microphone with him. I asked him if by any chance he recalled our first meeting at his mother's house.

"I thought it was in my apartment," he said, "But, yes, I do."

I reminded him of the drink he had poured me and confessed to my own embarrassment. "I sure thought you Montreal intellectuals were a pretty fast-living bunch," I said.

He smiled that enigmatic smile. "And I," he said, "thought all you Toronto journalists were alcoholics."

Riding High

Throughout the election campaign, Trudeau was a man riding an endless wave of energy and excitement. Away from the crowds, however, his shyness caused him to experience bouts of stage fright only minutes before he would dazzle a crowd with a rousing speech. A bachelor at forty-eight, Trudeau also battled with the strains the election placed on his privacy. Shortly after winning the Liberal leadership in April, he vowed, "I will not let this job louse up my private life." But with fewer than two weeks left in the election campaign, Trudeau almost tarnished his public shine.

On June 15, Liberal Party president John Nichol and Marc Lalonde met with Trudeau to persuade him not to cancel a tour of a number of western cities scheduled during the second-last week of the campaign. In Trudeau's chauffeur-driven vehicle, an argument among the three men became so heated that an RCMP officer was forced to inquire if everything was all right. At 24 Sussex Drive, Trudeau vaulted in frustration from the parked car towards the mansion where he said to Nichol "God damn you. I'll go."

Like all good actors, Trudeau knew his role well. He feared the stage, yet was a willing performer; he longed for privacy, but appeared most comfortable in a crowd; reason and logic governed his disposition, but his actions invited a frenzy of emotionalism unparalleled in Canadian political history.

Tru-deau-au-pot-eau

Long before 1968, the celebration of Saint-Jean-Baptiste Day on June 24 had become a Québécois day of pride, featuring beautifully decorated parade floats winding their way through the province's streets as citizens in costumes revelled in the festivities (ABOVE RIGHT). When Trudeau came to power, the festival took on a decidedly political tone.

The 1968 festivities were scheduled for the day before Canada went to the polls. As part of Montreal's ceremonies, organizers of the Saint-Jean-Baptiste parade invited Trudeau (ABOVE LEFT) to sit in the stands set out in front of the city's Bibliothèque municipale along with other dignitaries. Trouble began to brew when separatist movements, including the Reassemblement pour l'indépendance nationale (RIN), learned of Trudeau's intended presence and announced, "We will use all the means necessary to prevent Trudeau's plan."

At 9:30 p.m., the parade began to wind down Montreal's Sherbrooke Street. Sporadic clashes broke out between police and separatist elements within the half-million celebrants, but the procession itself remained unscathed. Then, around 10:30 p.m., a mob of 1,000 RIN-led separatists began chanting, Tru-deau-au-pot-eau! (Trudeau to the gallows!) and started throwing bottles – some filled with acid, kerosene, or paint – towards the stage. After a barrage of bottles hit the platform, Trudeau's bodyguard forced the prime minister to the ground as other spectators cleared the viewing area. In an act of defiance, Trudeau shook his fist at the guard and resumed his front-row seat.

For a brief period, the television cameras caught the image of Trudeau alone facing the chants of Quebec separatists. Within minutes, most of the province's other leaders returned, but not before news flashes of the prime minister's solitary stance were transmitted to the nation's television screens. Although the separatists continued to riot long into the evening (OPPOSITE), their real damage was to their own cause. The following morning, Canadians went to the polling booths along with the prime minister (LEFT) with the image of the cool and courageous Trudeau still fresh in their minds. Of the 264 seats in the House of Commons, the Liberals won 155, enough for the first majority government in six years.

Into Control

Trudeau and members of his newly sworn-in cabinet (ABOVE, LEFT TO RIGHT) — James Richardson, D.C. Jamieson, John Turner, Jean Marchand, and Gérard Pelletier – strut towards Parliament. Among the early steps taken by Trudeau to improve the efficiency of government were spending cutbacks, as presented by the prime minister (TOP ROW, LEFT). As well, Trudeau, along with Gérard Pelletier and Jean Marchand, seen here in the dining room at 24 Sussex Drive (TOP ROW, MIDDLE), took measures to provide French Canadians with equal opportunities. In October 1968, the Official Languages Act was presented to the House of Commons, outlining the Liberals' intention to create a fully bilingual federal government. Another change implemented by the Liberals was to lower the national voting age from twenty-one to eighteen; this ensured that a higher number of Canadians had a voice in government (TOP ROW, RIGHT).

In an effort to increase Canadian unity, early attempts were made to protect Canada from the growing influences of American culture. In 1970, the Canadian Radio-television and Telecommunications Commission (CRTC) began hearing pleas from members of the media, including Pierre Berton (SECOND ROW, LEFT), E.S. Hallman, Laurent A. Picard, George F. Davidson (SECOND ROW, MIDDLE), and Adrienne Clarkson (SECOND ROW, RIGHT) to impose stricter regulations on the amount of American content in the media.

The frustrations experienced by aboriginal groups in the late 1960s over the government's shifting Indian Affairs policy review prompted Harold Cardinal (THIRD ROW, LEFT), the president of the Indian Association of Alberta (IAA), to publish *The Unjust Society: The Tragedy of Canada's Indians* in 1969. Several months later, the *Red Paper*, a recommendation to transfer a number of federal powers directly to native groups, was presented to Northern Affairs Minister Jean Chrétien and Prime Minister Trudeau (THIRD ROW, MIDDLE) by IAA representatives including Chief Walter Deiter (THIRD ROW, RIGHT).

It was not long before other demonstrators began to reveal that Canada was not yet a just society. Although Trudeau's Omnibus Bill took steps towards legalizing abortion, women marched (FOURTH ROW, LEFT) against the law's requirement that a pregnancy must be life-threatening to the mother before an abortion could be performed legally. Shouts of racism, too, crept into Canada, after students at Montreal's Sir George Williams University destroyed the school's computer facilities (FOURTH ROW, MIDDLE) following racial accusations. For many, however, the love affair with the prime minister continued. After meeting Trudeau with her husband John Lennon (FOURTH ROW, RIGHT), Yoko Ono expressed the prime minister's persistent allure best: "It was a beautiful meeting. He is beautiful."

Descent into Terror

On October 5, 1970, British Trade Commissioner James Cross was kidnapped in Montreal by the Front de libération du Québec (FLQ). Since its founding in 1962, the FLQ, which described itself as "a group of Quebec workers who have decided to use all means to make sure that the people of Quebec take control of their own destiny", had become increasingly militant.

For the release of Cross, the FLQ demanded $500,000 and the return of twenty-three "political prisoners" being held for previous acts of terrorism including bombings, robbery, and murder. Trudeau refused to enter into negotiations with the FLQ. He believed that acknowledgement of the terrorists would only incite further acts of escalated violence, causing the government to be held hostage by a hostile faction.

Only five days after Cross was attacked, Pierre Laporte, a respected Quebec minister and former Brébeuf schoolmate of Pierre Trudeau, was kidnapped in broad daylight in front of his Montreal home. Fearing mass civil disorder, Quebec Premier Robert Bourassa requested that Trudeau provide military assistance and invoke the War Measures Act. Under the National Defenses Act, the Canadian government is required to provide the services of the military upon the formal request of a province's attorney general. Within days Trudeau met this obligation by assigning 10,000 soldiers to the streets of Montreal, Ottawa (BELOW), and residences of politicians and diplomats (CENTRE). For now, however, he refused to implement the War Measures Act.

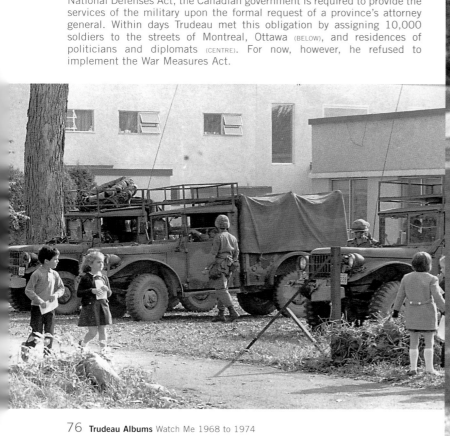

Just Watch Me

After the kidnapping of Pierre Laporte, Robert Bourassa called Trudeau almost daily to request that the federal government implement the War Measures Act. The prime minister continued to deny Bourassa's request.

Trudeau's stance changed dramatically on October 15, when *Le Devoir* printed a full-page document signed by sixteen leading Quebec business, academic, trade-union, and political leaders, including René Lévesque and Claude Ryan. The signatories requested the federal government's "urgent support in negotiating an exchange between hostages and political prisoners." The fact that these leaders viewed imprisoned members of a terrorist group as "political prisoners" told Trudeau that the situation was out of control. When a reporter asked the prime minister how far he was prepared to go to fight against what he called "a parallel power which sets itself against the elected," he replied, "Just watch me." On October 16, Trudeau invoked the War Measures Act.

The FLQ, in retaliation to the government's strong measures, ruthlessly killed Pierre Laporte. On October 17, his body was found in the trunk of a green Chevrolet parked at Montreal's St.-Hubert airport (TOP LEFT). By the time Trudeau and Bourassa attended Laporte's funeral on October 21 (BELOW), the FLQ independence-through-terror project had lost public sympathy. For the next two months, the police continued to enforce the War Measures Act. Eventually, the captors of James Cross, including the brothers Paul Rose (MIDDLE LEFT) and Jacques Rose (MIDDLE RIGHT), were arrested, but not before over 400 other Québécois were held by police for over forty-eight hours with no charges laid.

To bow to the pressures of these kidnappers who demand that the prisoners be released would be not only an abdication of responsibility, it would lead to an increase in terrorist activities in Quebec. It would be as well an invitation to terrorism and kidnapping across the country. We might well find ourselves facing an endless series of demands for the release of criminals from jails, from coast to coast, and we would find that the hostages could be innocent members of your family or of your neighbourhood. At the moment the FLQ is holding hostage two men in the Montreal area, one a British diplomat, the other a Quebec cabinet minister. They are threatened with murder. Should governments give into this crude blackmail, we would be facing the breakdown of the legal system and its replacement by the law of the jungle.

PIERRE ELLIOTT TRUDEAU | CBC TELEVISION ADDRESS | OCTOBER 16, 1970

The Dating Game

Pierre Trudeau was instantly elevated to the status of Canada's most eligible bachelor after becoming prime minister in 1968. Already well established in Montreal's singles scene, his star now rose to new heights. Margaret Sinclair, the daughter of James Sinclair, a member of the Liberal elite and former fisheries minister under Louis St. Laurent, first met Trudeau in 1967 while she was on a family vacation in Tahiti. Initially attracted to his athletic prowess, she later confessed, "I followed his progress idly, more than a little impressed by the ease of his performance."

In 1969, the two met again in Vancouver (OPPOSITE) while Trudeau was on a quick tour of the city. Shortly after the visit, Margaret moved to Ottawa where, through her father's connections, she found a job in the civil service and maintained contact with Trudeau. Not easily swayed by the efforts of a twenty-year-old, the prime minister made frequent headlines by escorting glamorous women, including Mademoiselle L. Marceau (BOTTOM LEFT) and Barbra Streisand (BOTTOM RIGHT). Eventually, Margaret's persistence won the day. On March 4, 1971, the couple surprised the nation when they announced their marriage (RIGHT) at a private Catholic ceremony in Vancouver. Despite the age difference between the fifty-one-year-old Trudeau and twenty-two-year-old Sinclair, many felt it was a perfect match.

The Campaign

In 1972, the Liberals faced another federal election. After assessing his diminished political power, the prime minister jokingly likened himself to Napoleon (CENTRE), and laughingly stated that he would pursue a course of action similar to the one followed by the French emperor at the Battle of Austerlitz.

Going into the election, Trudeau treated the 1972 campaign "not so much as an election battle as a simple appeal to the voters." Unlike the 1968 campaign, in which the Liberal strategists encouraged the prime minister to ride the wave of Trudeaumania, this campaign was more sober. Trudeau made a decision to approach voters and tell them, "Here's what we've accomplished in the past four years, and here are our plans for the next four years. If you like them, if you approve of them, then vote for us." Despite the bountiful efforts of youthful supporters (BELOW) to rejuvenate the spirit of 1968, Trudeau remained resolute in his approach. In the end, the Liberal strategy was lacklustre and was further challenged by the party's chosen slogan, "The Land Is Strong." Intended to inspire notions of national unity, the inept phrase was untranslatable into French.

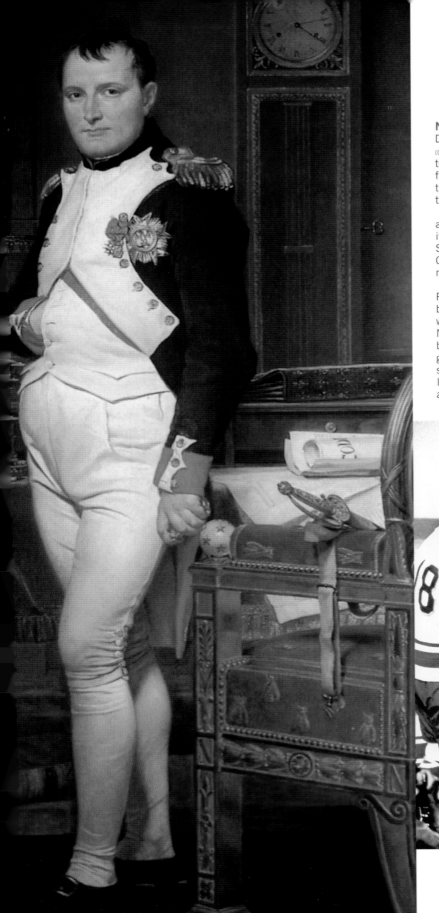

Napoleon and Me

David Lewis (OPPOSITE, TOP RIGHT), leader of the NDP, and Robert Stanfield (OPPOSITE, TOP LEFT), leader of the Conservatives, attacked Trudeau's approach to governing throughout the 1972 campaign. Lewis, hitting the Liberals from the left, accused the party of supporting "corporate welfare bums" through tax incentives and subsidies. Stanfield, meanwhile, pushing from the right, accused Trudeau of practising "chicken socialism."

Despite their weak campaign, early on the morning of October 31, Trudeau and the Liberal Party could breathe a sigh of relief. The government had lost its majority, but managed to hold on to power by a mere two seats over Stanfield's Conservatives. The Liberals, unlike Paul Henderson and Team Canada (BELOW), who had courageously defeated the Soviets in Moscow two months before, would have to be modest in their victory.

In the Battle of Austerlitz, faced with two enemy forces, Austria and Russia, Napoleon was forced to make a strategic retreat before doubling back on his opponents. After leading one army into a swamp, the French were able to annihilate each of their pursuers in turn. Trudeau's version of Napoleon's epic battle began in mid-December 1972, when he earned the backing of the NDP. To entice Lewis's continued support, the Liberal government, from 1972 until 1974, implemented a number of progressive social policies. The cost of the government's incentives was high, however. In each year of the minority government, the Liberals increased spending a staggering 20 percent.

1973 | China

Me and Mao

A major shift in Canada's foreign policy during Trudeau's first years in office was the establishment of diplomatic relations between Canada and the People's Republic of China. Only the second major Western nation, after France, to recognize the PRC – rather than Taiwan – as the official government of mainland China, Canada helped pave the way for other countries to follow suit.

While on a state visit to China in October 1973, Pierre and Margaret Trudeau enjoyed the beauty of the state opera (BELOW) and a panoramic view of the Chinese countryside (TOP CENTRE), in addition to demonstrations of Tai Chi (BOTTOM CENTRE). Although at the time of Trudeau's official state visit to China, Chairman Mao Zedong's ailing health greatly reduced his public appearances, portraits of his face (OPPOSITE, TOP) still hung everywhere. Trudeau, having heard that Mao still had lucid periods, was quietly hopeful that he might meet China's revolutionary leader for a second time in his life. (He first met Mao in 1960.) The prime minister's hopes were realized when, in the middle of a meeting with President Chou En-lai, Trudeau was suddenly whisked away to an unscheduled appointment with Chairman Mao in the Forbidden Palace.

Accompanying Trudeau on his state visit to China was Margaret (OPPOSITE, BOTTOM LEFT), pregnant with the couple's second child after only two and a half years of marriage. In the early days of her marriage, Margaret looked forward to travelling to exotic lands as the wife of the prime minister. However, the tiresome small talk and endless formalities of official duties soon shattered her early aspirations. On a state visit to Japan in 1976, she would yell "Fuck you!" to her husband in front of a number of dignitaries. For now, though, she maintained her composure and captured the attention of her Chinese admirers (OPPOSITE, BOTTOM RIGHT).

Into the Storm

The 1973 summer Western Conference, attended by British Columbia Premier Dave Barrett, Manitoba Premier Ed Schreyer, Pierre Trudeau, and Saskatchewan Premier Allan Blakeney (TOP LEFT, FROM LEFT TO RIGHT) was a bilateral meeting between Prime Minister Trudeau and the premiers of Canada's western provinces. Held in Calgary, it was an unprecedented political event: for the first time in Canadian history, the federal government entered into exclusive negotiations with a single region in Canada.

In the 1972 federal election, the total number of Liberal seats held in the west had been reduced from twenty-five to seven. Dave Barrett summed up Ottawa's change in policy to the tune of "Old MacDonald Had a Farm," "Here a vote, there a vote, everywhere a vote, vote." Although the issues on the negotiating table, which included unfair rail subsidies, interprovincial tariffs, and the centralization of chartered banks in eastern Canada, remained subjects of discussion after the conference was completed, the talks did set the tone for future rounds of regionally based discussions.

Lougheed, Lévesque, and King Khalid
Relations between Peter Lougheed (OPPOSITE, RIGHT), Alberta's Conservative premier, and the federal government soon soured after the Organization of Petroleum Exporting Countries, including Saudi Arabian King Khalid (ABOVE, IN CENTRE), repeatedly raised the price of oil in late 1973. Trudeau's response to the crisis was to implement a national oil policy, which provided Canadians with prices lower than those of the world market. These measures were taken without first consulting the Alberta government, an oversight that Lougheed would not quickly forget. While the western provinces stated their grievances with Ottawa, the Parti Québécois, led by René Lévesque (OPPOSITE, BOTTOM LEFT) continued to gain popularity with the Quebec electorate. In the June 1973 provincial election, Lévesque's party won 30.8 percent of the popular vote, although it took only six seats in the National Assembly.

Domestic Malaise
1974 to 1980

Domestic Malaise | Anne Kingston

T WAS FITTING THAT THE INDELIBLE IMAGE OF Pierre Elliott Trudeau's humiliating fall from power on May 22, 1979, was not of him. No. The photograph transmitted around the world the day after the Conservative Party victory was of his estranged wife, Margaret, giddily kicking up her heels in the camera-flash glare at New York City's Studio 54 hours after his defeat.

The focus on Margaret was apt. The most seditious political wife since Catherine the Great, Margaret had managed to eclipse her husband in a ceaseless campaign of self-revelation and defiant cuckoldry that spanned continents.

The prime minister's wife's ongoing public display of marital disillusionment, a five-year soap opera, had come to mirror the disenchantment the public felt towards her husband. Her frenzied dance-floor machinations echoed a national sentiment: we are free of him, free of him, free of him.

The political had become personal. Chaos in the Trudeau household was a neat metaphor for disorder in the Trudeau government. Had Pierre Trudeau been defeated by the OPEC crisis, worsening national unity, economic malaise, and scandals within the Liberal Party? Or was it more basic than that? Had his loss come down to this timeless political verity: If a man cannot control his wife, how can he control a government?

Five years is all it had taken for the centre to come undone. In 1974, Pierre Trudeau's choice of wife seemed inspired, his grip on the country's leadership assured. The Canadian public was taken aback by Trudeau's surprise marriage to Margaret Sinclair in March 1971, but there was no reason they should have known. In the early pre-Watergate 70s, the mainstream media maintained a hands-off policy towards politicians' personal lives. Scandal was the *amuse-gueule*, not yet the main course.

Press treatment of the wedding was respectful, authorized. There had no been no quizzing of Margaret's old boyfriends for dirt. The *Canadian* magazine ran five pages of posed photographs, followed by a feature on New Brunswick Premier Richard Hatfield, titled "Don't Cry, There's Still Richard Hatfield." The pairing of the 22-year-old bourgeois flower child and the 51-year-old intellectual was unlikely, but sense was made of it. She was young, yes, but so was he, at heart. Her father, James Sinclair, had been a Liberal cabinet minister, which was taken as reassurance that she understood the trade-offs of political life.

Margaret, who converted to Catholicism before the wedding, showed every sign of becoming the dutiful wife. Her domesticity was much discussed: imagine, she sewed her own caftan-styled wedding dress, even baked the wedding cake. There was also an unspoken relief that the bachelor prime minister was finally settling down; for a politician, a wife is a requirement, an anchor, evidence of stability. But Margaret Sinclair Trudeau was unlike other Canadian political wives. They were grey, voiceless accessories, subject to only the most cursory media scrutiny. Margaret was fresh, radiant. A nation mused, could she be our Jacqueline Bouvier Kennedy? and united in welcoming the

The Margaret Factor

Margaret Trudeau (OPPOSITE) stands in the spotlight during the 1974 federal election campaign. At the outset of the campaign Margaret had insisted on taking a public role, but was discouraged by Trudeau and the party strategists Keith Davey and Jim Coutts. She persevered, and was finally offered an opportunity to speak to an audience of 2,500 in West Vancouver. Standing before her hometown supporters, Margaret nervously described Trudeau as "a beautiful guy" who "taught me a lot about loving." To Davey and Coutts it looked as though their pre-election instincts were correct: Margaret, while hauntingly beautiful, was too unpredictable. Canadians, however, immediately fell in love with the prime minister's wife, and the "Margaret factor" became one of the campaign's primary attributes.

Enamoured with the public attention, the extroverted twenty-five-year-old "even dreamed of running in the next election," as she would later confess in her 1979 autobiography, *Beyond Reason*.

On July 8, 1974, the country re-elected Pierre Trudeau and his Liberals, who reclaimed a majority government. Margaret enjoyed one final campaign appearance at the party's election headquarters in the ballroom of Ottawa's Château Laurier Hotel. The next day the prime minister returned his attention to running the country, and the media shifted its focus to other stories and celebrities du jour. Left unattended at 24 Sussex and feeling used, Margaret later said, "Something in me broke that day."

ravishing woman who appeared a fitting consort to the country's first telegenic prime minister, a man whose face, a few years earlier, had adorned posters in Canadian teenaged girls' bedrooms.

Marshall McLuhan spoke of Trudeau's wizardry in pulling off "the transformation of the whole political scene into a marriage feast." The media's honeymoon with the couple continued. There was a triumphant tour of the Soviet Union. Two boys, Justin and Sacha, were born in quick succession, both on Christmas Day, which was taken as an omen, an indeterminate omen of some kind of divine nativity, but an omen nonetheless.

To the Toronto Liberal strategists plotting the 1974 spring election campaign, Margaret, as the beautiful, devoted young wife and mother, was a political asset. Pure gold. She grounded Trudeau yet gave him vitality; she made him appear to be in touch with the baby-boom generation. She was pushed front and centre, where she charmed, speaking of how her husband had taught her about love. She stood before the crowds, heartbreakingly sincere, the daisy tucked into the bandanna around her neck an echo of the flowers she had tucked in her hair for her wedding. News commentators began to discuss the positive effect of the "Margaret factor" on the campaign.

There was no reason then to think that the Trudeau marriage had drifted. The veneer was intact. Later, it would be told that she was restless; he, disillusioned by her demands and impetuousness. Later, the country would learn that Margaret, buoyed by the attention accorded her during the campaign, actually thought of running for office herself. Later, she would write in her memoir *Beyond Reason* that on the morning after the election that swept the Liberals in with a majority, she sat in her "freedom room" at 24 Sussex, "feeling that I had been used" and that "something in me broke that day."

Slowly, life behind the closed doors of 24 Sussex trickled into the public domain. The Watergate scandal had created a climate of cynicism towards the political process. Politicians and their foibles were fair quarry. Journalists began to see themselves as creating the story, not merely reporting it.

In September 1974, it was revealed that Margaret had been admitted to Montreal's Royal Victoria Hospital for what a press release from the PMO later referred to as "severe emotional stress." Shortly thereafter, in an unprecedented move, the prime minister's wife appeared on television to talk about how difficult and constraining she found the role to be.

In 1975, a third son, Michel, was born, and Margaret took up photography. It was International Women's Year, so it seemed fitting, fashionable even, that the prime minister's wife should want a small career for herself. And photography was an appropriately passive vocation: Linda Eastman had taken pictures before marrying Paul McCartney; Jacqueline Bouvier had been a photographer before her wedding to John Kennedy.

The imagery surrounding the Trudeau marriage remained upbeat. A photograph widely published in 1976 showed the Trudeaus joyously swinging their son Sacha between them in Vancouver airport on their way to an official visit to Japan. It wasn't widely reported that, in a public argument in Tokyo,

On the Campaign Trail

Following his near defeat in 1972, Trudeau enlisted the support of Liberal strategists Keith Davey (TOP LEFT) and Jim Coutts (TOP RIGHT), former key advisers to Lester Pearson. Over the course of the minority government, Coutts, Davey, and their team of political strategists convinced Trudeau to accept the NDP's demands for progressive legislation. And so it was that, by the spring of 1974, Trudeau had earned back the country's support in the polls. Eager to regain a majority government, the Liberals used Finance Minister John Turner's May 6 federal budget to orchestrate their own defeat in the House of Commons. As predicted, the Conservatives and the NDP rejected Turner's budget in a parliamentary vote of non-confidence, and the Liberals had their election.

On the campaign trail, Trudeau (BELOW) denounced Stanfield's proposed wage and price controls, effectively placing his opponent on the defensive. "We are going on the attack," Trudeau told Liberal supporters early in the campaign. And over the course of the next six weeks they did just that, eventually winning 141 of the 264 seats in the House of Commons.

Living in the Seventies

In 1970 Trudeau addressed Liberals about what the decade would bring Canadians (ABOVE LEFT). No predictions were made, however, about United States President Richard Nixon, who resigned on August 8, 1974, to avoid impeachment after the Watergate scandal. Instrumental in reducing pollution emissions along the waterway, Nixon (ABOVE MIDDLE) signed the Canada-U.S. Great Lakes Quality Agreement with Trudeau in April 1972.

Another high-stakes controversy of the 1970s featured Montreal's Dr. Henry Morgentaler (ABOVE RIGHT) as staunch defendant in one of the most divisive legal cases in Canadian history: women's right to receive abortions on demand. Morgentaler, who admitted to conducting more than 5,000 illegal abortions, took his case to the Supreme Court of Canada, which on March 26, 1974, upheld the Quebec Court of Appeal's decision to overturn his acquittal. He would later serve ten months of an eighteen-month sentence before a second jury acquitted him and all charges were dropped.

The United Nations declared 1975 to be International Women's Year. To mark the event the federal government commissioned photographer John

---

Margaret had yelled a very unwifely "fuck you" at her husband.

Soon, her erratic behaviour became impossible to conceal. The cameras were ever-present. At a formal dinner in Venezuela, she broke into a song to thank her hostess. On an official trip to Cuba, she wore a sheer Liberal Party T-shirt with nothing underneath it and flirted with Fidel Castro.

At the 1976 Olympics she was notably absent, AWOL, thrusting Pierre Trudeau into the role of single father. There was sympathy for his plight, but also impatience. This was not the imagery Canadians had elected.

By 1977, when the Trudeaus embarked on a trial separation, the carefully constructed mask of the marriage had been ripped away. It was discovered that Margaret stayed at the same hotel as the Rolling Stones the night following a Toronto concert. It was even rumoured she was having an affair with one of them. Which one? Ron Wood? Mick Jagger?

The Trudeau marriage became a guessing game, a sideshow more engaging than dreary domestic news of mounting inflation, rising unemployment and dissension in Quebec. Margaret was custom-ordered for the confessional age, unlike her Jesuit-schooled husband, who refused to comment on things personal. She was adopted into a burgeoning celebrity class of those famous for being famous.

For a brief time, she became a stringer photographer for *People*, the mass-market scripture of celebrity puffery, which began publication in 1974. Margaret Trudeau capitalized on her connections as the prime minister's wife to get the job. When it was discovered that she couldn't secure the access she had promised, the magazine let her go.

Other dalliances, including a stab at movie stardom, were equally brief. She was photographed frequently, often dancing frenetically, usually at Studio 54, home of the new one-name glitterati: Liza, Calvin, Halston, Andy, Bianca. Public sentiment swung to Pierre Trudeau, then away. His ability to govern had been thrown into doubt. He had introduced wage and price controls after opposing them in the 1974 election. He had lost control of the Quebec agenda, first to Robert Bourassa, then to René Lévesque, elected Quebec premier in 1976. It was said Trudeau's pride prevented him from confiding in colleagues, that he was distracted by the emotional turmoil of his personal life.

The marriage. Analysis of it came to serve as a gloss on his character, particularly by Quebecers. How telling, in retrospect, that he had married an English-Canadian girl. How ironic that the man who fought so passionately for a centralized government couldn't keep his own family together. Years later, Christina McCall Newman and Stephen Clarkson wrote in *Trudeau and Our Times: The Magnificent Obsession* that the marriage had further pumped up Trudeau's "sense of omnipotence." "It must have seemed as

Reeves to capture images of Canadian women, among whom was Margaret Atwood (ABOVE LEFT), a respected international voice in Canadian literature. On July 30, 1974, the Quebec Liberal Party, led by Premier Robert Bourassa (ABOVE MIDDLE), passed Bill 22, making French the official language of Quebec. Bourassa's unilingual stance came at a time when many English Canadians were still skeptical about Trudeau's vision of a bilingual Canada.

Following the 1974 election a restless Margaret Trudeau (ABOVE RIGHT) travelled first to Europe for two weeks in search of an ex-lover, then to New York where she fell in love with American Senator Edward Kennedy. After Trudeau confronted Margaret about her behaviour she threatened suicide, which led to her stay at Montreal's Royal Victoria Hospital for "emotional problems." Back at Sussex Drive, the prime minister's wife was given greater freedom, including her own car, a private phone line, and permission to travel and study photography.

though he could have everything that befitted a hero: the power, the sagacity, and the stable family life that comes with middle age along with the optimism and spontaneity of youth."

But that was not how it appeared on the cusp of the 1979 spring election. By then, the "Margaret factor" had turned against Pierre Trudeau. *Beyond Reason*, the first of Margaret's two memoirs, was released to a tumult of publicity. In it, she wrote of the misery that was her marriage, of her husband being inflexible and self-contained, of her suicide attempts, of smoking marijuana at 24 Sussex under the nose of the RCMP. She claimed that he had hit her.

The May election was a rout for the Liberals. Yet echoes of the man Canadians had voted into office in 1968 began to emerge. After formally tendering his resignation as prime minister to Governor General Schreyer, he drove himself away from Rideau Hall in a Mercedes convertible sports car he had not been seen in since 1968, when he was the debonair bachelor prime minister. Photographers captured him vaulting into the front seat and driving away alone, as if for the last time, as if there were no surprises left.

That summer, Trudeau set off on a personal pilgrimage to Tibet and China, returning with a beard, a new man. Yet the wife problem remained. In an interview that ran in the September *Playgirl*, Margaret chronicled her affairs with famous men. She spoke of longing to have singer Lou Rawls's baby. That month,

High Society magazine ran a photograph of her sitting on the floor of Studio 54, clearly not wearing panties. Inside was an article titled "Maggie Trudeau: Canada's Loose Leading Lady."

On November 21, three days before the annual Liberal executive meeting, Pierre Trudeau announced his resignation as Opposition Leader. A month later, prodded by a new slate of Liberal strategists led by Keith Davey and Jim Coutts, he reversed that decision. By then, as the pollsters had calculated, the country had wearied of Margaret's antics.

Margaret had not kept her part of the political-wife covenant. She had not redecorated or fronted for noble charities. She had not been voiceless. She had defied her husband and her marital vows. It was suggested she was suffering from some form of mental illness. But Canadian political wives were proving to be a feisty lot. The Conservative Leader Joe Clark's wife, Maureen McTeer, raised public vexation by insisting on keeping her maiden name and pursuing a law career.

Public sympathy was shifting again in Pierre Trudeau's favour. The movie *Kramer vs. Kramer*, which made a hero of the single, abandoned father, had just been released. The country was ready for something new, even if that something new was a resurrected version of the singular man who had captured its imagination more than a decade before. Yes. The lens, at last, was back on Pierre Elliott Trudeau.

Security and Isolation

"The Just Society will be one in which those regions and groups which have not fully shared in the country's affluence will be given a better opportunity," declared a newly elected Trudeau in June 1968. But after three federal elections and six years in office, Trudeau seemed to be moving away from his early political ideals. The prime minister – posed (OPPOSITE) with Margaret and sons Justin and Sacha in 1974 – was increasingly regarded as being incapable of understanding the everyday challenges faced by middle- and lower-class Canadians. He had grown up in a privileged family, lived in a privileged neighbourhood, and attended privileged schools. Shortly after regaining a majority government, Trudeau authorized the construction of a $200,000 indoor pool for 24 Sussex Drive.

During a CBC television interview with Trudeau in October 1976, Barbara Frum put it to him this way: "I don't know if anyone says this quite to your face. A lot of Canadians don't think you understand them because you are privileged yourself, you are secure yourself. That's a very isolating thing for a hard time." To which Trudeau replied, "Well ... I'm ... you know, a prime minister is secure. He's got policemen around him and he's got a house to live in and he's got a car. In that sense, all prime ministers have been no less secure than me. But what you call isolated, do you know any prime minister who has travelled more than I in the country, and met more groups more often?"

Between 1974 and 1976 public hostility towards Trudeau increased as "stagflation" – the simultaneous increase in unemployment and inflation – grew worse. In the Maritime provinces the hardships were particularly gruelling. As this Prince Edward Island family (LEFT) exemplifies, despite Trudeau's early initiatives to transfer massive tax revenues from richer provinces to poorer regions through the Department of Regional Economic Expansion (DREE), many Canadian citizens were not living in a "just society."

The Liberal government, which had so strongly campaigned against Robert Stanfield's proposed wage and price controls during the 1974 campaign, appeared to be turning a blind eye to the country's economic problems. In one of his first public speeches following the July election, Trudeau talked about bilingualism, continued parliamentary reforms, and the Constitution. The pressing issue of inflation was relegated to his conclusion, in which he remarked, "There are other subjects I could deal with. Native rights ... the status of women ... um .... inflation."

Federal Portfolio

In 1971 the Trudeau government established the Canadian Development Corporation (CDC), a holding company for its investment in such strategic industries as energy, transportation, and communication. As a result the federal government's corporate portfolio ballooned in the 1970s and early 1980s, adding the likes of Petro Canada, de Havilland, Canadair, VIA Rail, and Canada Post Corporation to the nation's more traditional crown holdings such as the Canadian National Railways (BELOW), which became a crown corporation in 1917. For its part, the Quebec government under Premier Jean Lesage had de-privatized the province's hydroelectric industry in the 1960s. This bid to reduce Quebec's dependence on foreign capital saw the creation of such works as the controversial James Bay hydroelectric power development (RIGHT), launched in 1971.

Up to Bat

While it may have appeared that the prime minister was prepared to give Canadians the shirt off his back (BELOW), he was actually dressing to play in a baseball game on Parliament Hill. Not long after his 1974 victory, Trudeau's showmanship was wearing thin. His support had fallen to a mere 29 percent in the polls, and Canadians, like this protester (LEFT), were beginning to show signs of their disenchantment.

Frustrated with the government's economic initiatives, John Turner, Liberal minister of finance, resigned on September 10, 1975. The sudden loss of one of the most highly respected federal ministers sent shock waves through the Canadian business world. One month later, Trudeau announced the implementation of wage and price controls in a nationally televised address. His 1974 election jab at Stanfield's proposed controls – "a proven disaster looking for a new place to happen" – had come back to haunt him.

Viva Cuba

"Viva Cuba y el pueblo cubano. Viva el Primer Ministro Comandante Fidel Castro. Viva la amistad cubano-canadiense" (Long live Cuba and the Cuban People. Long live Prime Minister and Commander Fidel Castro. Long live Cuban-Canadian friendship), shouted Pierre Trudeau in passable Spanish to a crowd of 25,000 Cubans at the start of his three-day visit to the Caribbean island in January 1976. When Pierre and Margaret Trudeau arrived at Havana's José Marti airport they were greeted enthusiastically by thousands of Cubans (OPPOSITE). The visit sparked Cuban hopes that the Western world would soon recognize their country. Cuba's friendship, spelled out in the signs along the crowd's perimeter, was a genuine display of its appreciation for Canada's continued diplomatic relations with Castro's government. Despite their ideological differences, Trudeau and Castro shared an admiration for each other. "I'd rate him A-1. All kinds of superlatives," Trudeau told a Havana press conference. Margaret, not to be outdone by her husband, made headlines of her own by donning a form-fitting Liberal T-shirt (ABOVE) at one of the couple's scheduled appearances. In a March 1977 *People* magazine interview Margaret would reveal how world leaders had reacted to the outline of her nipples visible through her clothes.

The Trudeaus' trip to Cuba was complicated by the country's involvement in Angola's civil war. Castro had assured Trudeau that the number of Cuban troops on Angolan soil was minimal, and that they were there only for the interim. The two leaders concluded the three-day visit with an amicable bear hug. Upon returning to Ottawa, Trudeau learned that there were many more Cuban troops in Angola than Castro had indicated and that their intended length of stay was indefinite. All Canadian foreign aid to Cuba, save humanitarian, was immediately halted.

1976 | Domestic Malaise

Final Swing

In February 1976 the time had come for the Progressive Conservatives to find a successor to their leader Robert Stanfield, the Nova Scotian politician who had fought diligently against Trudeau in three elections. After four ballots, thirty-six-year-old Joe Clark (RIGHT, WITH FLORA MACDONALD) won the party leadership. Brian Mulroney, the front-runner going into the convention, was forced to bow out after the third ballot. In his victory speech, Clark declared his intention to spend less time in the House of Commons and more time meeting Canadians.

In June, Quebec dairy farmers, upset by the government's reduction of subsidies and quotas, struck Agriculture Minister Eugene Whelan with a milk jug during a demonstration on Parliament Hill. Two years later, Saskatchewan dairy farmers would dump milk on the steps of the Regina legislature (BELOW) in a continued fight against the Liberals' unwillingness to grant greater assistance to Canada's dairy industry.

The very image of an apparently happy family, Trudeau and Margaret swing their son Sacha (OPPOSITE) through the airport before departing for Japan in October 1976. Several months earlier, after a spring poll indicated that only 20 percent of Quebecers supported separatism, Trudeau had triumphantly proclaimed "Separatism is dead." But René Lévesque would use the prime minister's words to convince Quebec voters that separatism was a non-issue in the province's upcoming election, promising that if elected he would strengthen Quebec's economy before considering further separatist options. On November 15, 1976, the Parti Québécois (BOTTOM) won the provincial election. It was a victory that stunned the nation. When Margaret Trudeau heard the results she burst into tears, certain that her husband "would never leave politics now." The Trudeaus separated six months later.

At Odds

The July 1976 Montreal Summer Olympics afforded Pierre Trudeau – with sons Sacha and Justin (ABOVE), watching the wrestling match (OPPOSITE) – an opportunity to enjoy being a spectator rather than the main event. In the months leading up to the Olympics, Trudeau's bilingual policies had met with mounting criticism throughout Canada. In March, Official Languages Commissioner Keith Spicer declared that Trudeau's attempts to integrate bilingualism into the federal government had failed: Anglo civil servants were refusing to use their newly learned French on the job, and a Gallup poll revealed that support for institutional bilingualism had fallen to an all-time low of 37 percent.

Adding jet fuel to the language conflagration was the *Gens de l'air* Affair, which erupted when the federal government proposed legislation that would give Quebec pilots the option of speaking French to air traffic controllers. Anglo pilots and controllers argued that the resulting risk of miscommunication would endanger the lives of all who flew over Canadian skies. Their ensuing nine-day strike was described by Trudeau as the worst threat to national unity since the Conscription Crisis.

The Montreal Olympics suffered its own political sting after twenty-two African nations withdrew from the games to protest the Olympic Committee's failure to expel New Zealand, which had recently sent a rugby team to play in South Africa. And, after all the medals were awarded and the final national anthem played, the 1976 Olympics' greatest legacy to Canadians was the $995 million deficit the games had accumulated.

Pirouette

Pierre Trudeau had an incredible talent for making the contrived look spontaneous. In what is arguably the best-known photograph (OPPOSITE) from his time in office, a poker-faced Trudeau performs a pirouette behind the back of Queen Elizabeth II during a reception at Buckingham Palace in May 1977. The glare of the spotlights reflected in a mirror confirms that Trudeau likely wanted to be caught by a photographer's lens. He had rehearsed the twirl – a gesture of his opposition to palace protocol that in his view separated the head of state from the heads of government – hours before in his hotel.

It was Trudeau's ability to perform that enabled him to remain outwardly dignified through the final turbulent months of his marriage. Anxious to find a career of her own, Margaret had attempted still photography before deciding to put herself in front of the camera – in the films *Kings and Desperate Men* and *L'Ange Guardien* (ABOVE). Yet Margaret would remain better known for the company she kept. The night of her sixth wedding anniversary found her at a Rolling Stones concert in Toronto, after which she was spotted in a hallway of the Stones' hotel wearing a white bathrobe. When asked to comment, Trudeau replied loftily, "I do not indulge in guilt by association."

On May 27, 1977, the prime minister's office issued a brief statement: "Pierre and Margaret Trudeau announce that because of Margaret's wishes, they shall begin living separate and apart. Margaret relinquishes all privileges as the wife of the Prime Minister and wishes to leave the marriage to pursue an independent career." The departure of his wife from 24 Sussex Drive made Trudeau the first single-parent prime minister in Canadian history.

Political Despair

Between 1977 and 1979 thousands of *"à vendre"* (for sale) signs appeared on Quebec buildings (ABOVE), as close to 100,000 anglophones left the province in the wake of escalating anti-English sentiment. In January 1978, Sun Life, the country's largest Canadian-owned insurance company, closed its offices in Montreal and decamped to Toronto. The Anglo exodus from Quebec had begun in the early seventies, but it wasn't until the August 1977 passage of the Parti Québécois's harsh language legislation, Bill 101, that an overwhelming number of English-speaking residents elected to leave la belle province.

A new series of Canadian political battle lines were drawn with the return to Iran of the exiled Ayatollah Khomeini (OPPOSITE) in February 1979. The political instability of the oil-rich nation created renewed fears of rapidly increasing oil prices in the Western world. For Alberta Premier Peter Lougheed, it presented an opportunity to negotiate with Ottawa on behalf of his province for a more favourable National Energy Program. When the federal government introduced the program in 1980, however, its interventionist policies would only intensify the conflict between Ottawa and the western provinces.

As the political climate in Canada continued to heat up, Trudeau became increasingly isolated from his party and from Canadians. Making policy decisions without consulting his cabinet, chiding demonstrators, and openly antagonizing any politician who dared oppose him, Trudeau's Liberal Party continued to fall out of favour.

Out of Touch

On March 26, 1979, Trudeau called a federal election for May 22 after learning that Margaret's tell-all book, *Beyond Reason*, was scheduled for release in April. Keith Davey urged him to extend his current mandate until July 8, the latest possible date he could call an election, but Trudeau knew that the longer he waited, the more Margaret would talk.

Despite a campaign that relied heavily on its leader, Trudeau appeared to forget those who supported him. While the nation wanted answers about its ailing economy, Trudeau focused on the Constitution. The 1979 campaign featured the first televised federal leaders' debate in Canadian history (BELOW). Conservative Leader Joe Clark (SEATED AT RIGHT) and NDP Leader Ed Broadbent (SEATED AT LEFT) used the opportunity to attack Trudeau's government. Clark asserted, "If there has been one fundamental political disease in the last eleven years, it is the sense that the government is going one way and the people are going another way – that there has been government by an isolated elite." The prime minister (SEATED IN THE CENTRE) appeared uninterested through much of the debate, but in its final moments he effortlessly picked apart Clark's weak stance on the Constitution and his inability to win complete support of the country's Tory premiers. Yet in the face of Trudeau's patently superior grasp of rhetoric Clark held his own, proving to be a stronger leader than the electorate had expected.

Cruel Disappointment

Jim Coutts (TOP, ON RIGHT), Keith Davey (MIDDLE LEFT), and other liberal strategists (MIDDLE BOTTOM) seemed suspended in shock at Liberal Party headquarters in the Château Laurier's ballroom on the night of May 22, 1979. Pierre Trudeau had been defeated by Joe Clark, whose Progressive Conservatives had won 136 seats in the House of Commons. After eleven years as prime minister, the country had rejected Trudeau and his vision of Canada.

On the morning of May 23, 1979, as Trudeau absorbed his election defeat, newspapers around the world carried an image (BELOW) of Margaret dancing frantically in New York's popular Studio 54 nightclub. "Wearin' my pink pedal pushers and my dancin' shoes ... I thought I could get over the cruel disappointment of it all ... if only I could smile and dance!" she said.

The important thing is that we haven't given up an inch on our principles as Liberals. We stood for minority rights as the Liberal Party always has and always will stand for minority rights in every part of this country. We've fought for equality of opportunity, we've put forth programs while we were the government and during the election campaign to ensure that equality would be even greater....We've fought also for something which I think extraordinarily important at this time in our history, that is a strong national government, and I believe we were right in that, and I still believe that that's the kind of government that not only this country deserves but that it needs at this time. And I want to say for those of you who were perhaps surprised to see me talk in the last weeks of the campaign about having a Canadian constitution made by Canadians, in Canada, for Canadians. I still think, I believe this was the right course, I knew that when I took that course we took the risk of failing greatly and perhaps we did in the short-run, but I'm absolutely certain, that in the medium and longer term, this is the course that Canada will have to follow .... With all its sham, drudgery and broken dreams, it's still a beautiful world, strive to be happy.

PIERRE ELLIOTT TRUDEAU | ELECTION NIGHT ADDRESS, OTTAWA | MAY 22, 1979

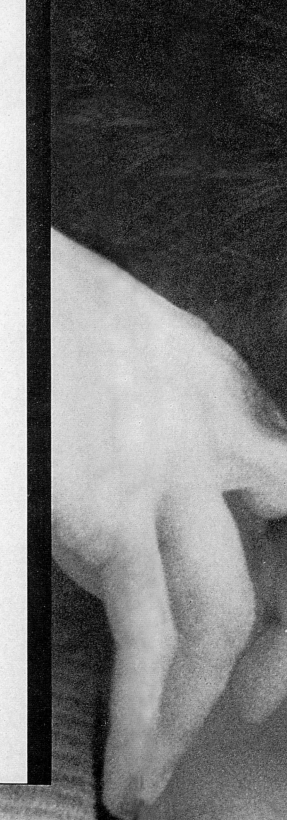

MARGARET TRUDEAU

A revealing conversation about her life with an older man (Pierre),
her closet boyfriend (Ryan), and why she'll always love Ted Kennedy.

"Ah'm in love for the first time. An' I know it's gonna la-a-a-ast."

It is a clear, sun-kissed Southern California afternoon, and Margaret Trudeau is running up the front steps of the Beverly Hills Hotel in her bright-red high heels, singing. Surprisingly, the hotel staff has not been the least bit annoyed with Margaret's usually less-than-decorous behavior. She's been livening the place up for more than a week, they say, so they'll be genuinely sorry to see her leave.

We are on our way to a clandestine rendezvous at the Polo Lounge with an old flame Margaret has just bumped into at a Jane Fonda solar-energy fund raiser.

Margaret stops suddenly. "We *can't* tell him you're a journalist. It'll freak him out." The Old Flame is a very well-known film actor who is famous for, among other things, his phobic aversion to the press. "What'll we tell him?"

"That I'm your yoga teacher," I say half-jokingly.

"*Perfect!*" says the estranged wife of the ex–prime minister of Canada. "Don't worry. It'll all be so much *fun.*"

Once upon a time, in the semimythological decade known as the sixties, there was a very pretty and very idealistic young Canadian woman named Margaret Sinclair. She did all the things the young and rebellious did in those days: She ate macrobiotically, talked revolution, and spent eight mescaline-high hours in a tree, willing herself to be a bird, and a season or two tripping the dope-strewn, mystical-hippie trail in Morocco.

"I must experience life firsthand," she explained to her horrified former–cabinet minister father.

The Christmas just after she turned nineteen, Margaret rejoined her family briefly in Tahiti where she met a nice, athletic, older chap named Pierre. When he asked her out she stood him up in favor of a younger, cosmic-speaking Frenchman. Pierre went on to become the prime minister of Canada, and Margaret went off to Marrakesh.

But eighteen months later, when Margaret was back in Canada (and mooning about the Frenchman), the prime minister took it upon himself to ring her up for a date. Star-struck and insecure, but curious, Margaret accepted. She told him about drugs and student activism. He told her to give him a call if she ever got to Ottawa. Margaret was barely twenty; Pierre was forty-nine.

The Old Flame is leering pleasantly across the table at Margaret. "Hey," he says, waggling his eyebrows suggestively, "you wanna come up and see my *Jacuzzi?*"

Margaret just shrieks with laughter. "Did you hear *that?* And this is supposed to be the man who has the best lines in Hollywood!"

The Old Flame looks sheepish. "Is anybody hungry?" he asks. Then, to the waiter, "Bring some of those hors d'oeuvres, you know, the shrimp things."

"Do you have caviar?" Margaret says, smiling her sweetest Zelda Fitzgerald smile. "I'd like just caviar, please. Nothing else." Yes, they have it, the waiter tells her, but the management requires him to inform us that the caviar is thirty dollars an ounce.

"Fine," says the Old Flame.

"Oh, *I'm* paying," says Margaret. "I've my pocket money right here in m'pocket. This lady pays her *own* way now."

Margaret moved to Ottawa the following month. And she did call Pierre. For the next

No Control

In the fall of 1979, two years after her separation from Trudeau, Margaret continued to shock the world. Soft-porn magazines, including *High Society* and *Playgirl* (LEFT), featured articles on the former prime minister's wife. In *High Society* a chance snapshot, taken as she prepared to autograph an admirer's notebook in a New York nightclub, revealed a skirt-wearing Margaret caught pantyless. Although *Playgirl's* interview with Margaret did not feature nudity, disclosures in the text were far more damning. She discussed her passion for celebrity love-making, the abortion she had undergone at seventeen, and the pleasure she took in publicizing details of her marriage. For Trudeau the humiliation was great. Pressed for an explanation, Margaret told him simply, "I'm sick. I know now there are situations in which I just cannot control myself."

Out of Office

Two weeks after his May election defeat, Trudeau drove his 1959 Mercedes 300SL to Rideau Hall to hand in his official resignation as Canada's prime minister (BELOW). "I have no regrets and no remorse," he told Governor General Ed Schreyer before bidding him farewell. "I feel free," he informed the press before speeding off to an uncertain future as leader of the Official Opposition.

Over the summer months Trudeau took to two of his greatest pleasures: canoeing and travel. The full beard (RIGHT) that he wore upon his return to Ottawa was a testament to his first taste of liberty since 1968. His principal secretary Jim Coutts advised, "If you want to give the signal that you are out for good, keep the beard. But if you think you might like to stay on, you damn well better shave it off."

Once Parliament was finally called into session in October 1979, the Right Honourable Pierre Trudeau proved to be at best a lacklustre opposition leader. After struggling through two months of debate in the House of Commons, where his absence was frequently noted, he announced his resignation on November 21, 1979.

Oui *ou* Non

In August 1979 Canada lost one of its greatest champions of unity with the death of John Diefenbaker, whose funeral train (BELOW) carried him from Ottawa to his final resting place in Saskatchewan. Diefenbaker, who remained a member of parliament until his death, had lived long enough to witness his party's return to power, but at a time when his dream of One Country was threatened by René Lévesque's campaign for Quebec sovereignty.

Shortly after Trudeau's resignation the Parti Québécois strategically announced its intention to hold a referendum the following spring on the province's separation from Canada. By the time the initial wording of the referendum question was read out in the province's National Assembly (LEFT) on December 20, however, Lévesque's fortunes had begun to change.

On December 13, 1979, Joe Clark's fledgling government was forced to call a federal election after Tory Finance Minister John Crosbie's federal budget was defeated in a vote of non-confidence. With the February 18, 1980, election only two months away, the Liberals could not afford the luxury of a lengthy leadership campaign. The obvious choice was Trudeau, but many within the party had lost confidence in him. Although tempted to confront Lévesque directly in Quebec's referendum, Trudeau insisted he would not return as Liberal leader unless he received support from all levels of the party. By December 17, Trudeau had been assured the support of the Liberal caucus, the party executive, and the majority of his closest friends and advisers. The decision now rested on his shoulders.

LA QUESTION

Accordez-vous au gouvernement du Québec le mandat de négocier l'entente proposée entre le Québec et le Canada? OUI – NON »

I'm Back | Mordecai Richler

4 58 B.C. IT WAS, WHEN CINCINNATUS famously abandoned his plough, quitting his farm to resume the dictatorship of the Holy Roman Empire, to put down the plebeians. In 1979 A.D., copycat Pierre Elliott Trudeau also came out of retirement, shaving off his beard and confining his nifty sports car to a garage again, to lead the Liberals back into power, smite the separatist dragon, repatriate the Constitution, and bestow a Charter of Rights and Freedoms on Canada. Alas, his Constitution was compromised, tainted by what my agent calls a "deal-breaker," the "notwithstanding clause," which enabled Quebec to impose fatuous restraints on the language of les maudits anglais. All the same, the period from 1980 to 1984 must be account-ed the most significant of the Trudeau years, leaving the country with a legacy that is still contentious, largely in Quebec, whose sulk-ing provincial politicians refused to agree to the Constitution Act of 1982, protesting date-rape by the notorious Gang of Eight.

"Welcome to the 1980s," a jubilant Trudeau proclaimed to a flock of adoring Liberals (returned to office, their divine right) in the Château Laurier on the night of February 18, 1980. With a little help from Keith Davey and Jim Coutts, a moxie duo, the Liberals had won 147 seats to 103 for the Tories, and 32 for the traditionally third-place NDP. Trudeau got his majority, but he had taken only two seats west of Ontario, and if you put your ear to the prairie soil you could just make out the rumbling of a former radio evangelist, Preston Manning, who was beginning to think secular. And soon enough, Canada would suffer the near-demise of the Tories and the rise of fulminating regional protest parties: the reformers out West and the Bloc Québécois in la belle province.

Trudeau was blessed in his anti-charismatic 1980 adversary, sincere Joe Clark, a fumbler born. Trudeau arrogantly dismissed him for acting as the head waiter to the provinces, advocating a Canada that would be a "community of communities," rather than a nation. Poor Joe. I can recall watching a TV debate between Trudeau, Ed Broadbent, and Joe, which struck me as being what boxing writers would have declared a mismatch, a contest between two men and a boy. Then Joe, whoring after the Jewish vote in Toronto, established forevermore his propensity for putting the puck into his own net by foolishly promising to move the Canadian embassy in Israel from Tel Aviv to Jerusalem. Later, he would send good soldier Robert Stanfield on a fool's errand – Stanfield would tour all the Arab capitals to test their reaction to Joe's proposal. To the amazement of only Joe Clark, the Arabs thought the idea was a bummer.

Trudeau hardly had the time to rearrange the furniture in 24 Sussex Drive, before the Parti Québécois, fearful, then as now, of daring a direct appeal to Quebecers on independence, surfaced with their murky, too-clever-by-half referendum question:

THE GOVERNMENT OF QUEBEC HAS MADE PUBLIC its proposal to negotiate a new agreement with the rest of Canada

Return to Power

"Welcome to the 1980s," proclaimed Prime Minister Pierre Trudeau on February 18, 1980. Exactly two months after he had re-entered the political arena determined to defeat Joe Clark's Conservatives and halt René Lévesque's efforts to create a sovereign Quebec, Trudeau had just won his fourth election victory.

The Liberals' election strategy – masterminded by veterans Jim Coutts and Keith Davey – had put the Conservatives on the defensive. Trudeau spoke out against the troubled mandate of Clark's nine-month government, highlighting its inability to negotiate an energy program with Alberta Premier Peter Lougheed and its failed effort to move the Canadian embassy in Israel from Tel Aviv to Jerusalem. During the campaign Trudeau kept a low profile, making only a select number of key appearances across the country. The Constitution, cornerstone of his 1979 election campaign, did not feature in his 1980 platform. Instead, Trudeau addressed the need for establishing a National Energy Program, increasing the role of the Foreign Investment Review Agency in regulating foreign ownership, and strengthening the automobile industry. The strategy was a success: the Liberals reaped 147 seats in the House of Commons, a decisive majority.

based on the equality of nations; this agreement would enable Quebec to acquire the exclusive power to make its laws, levy its taxes and establish relations abroad – in other words, sovereignty – and at the same time, to maintain with Canada an economic association including a common currency; no change in political status resulting from these negotiations will be effected without approval by the people through another referendum; on these terms, do you give the Government of Quebec the mandate to negotiate the proposed agreement between Quebec and Canada? Yes. No.

THE PARTI QUÉBÉCOIS'S REFERENDUM CAMPAIGN WAS ridden with gaffes. Take, for instance, the so-called "Yvette" incident. "[It] began," Trudeau wrote in his memoirs, "when a prominent female minister (Lise Payette) in Lévesque's Cabinet made the terrible blunder of mocking women who weren't out there fighting for separatism and instead were staying home minding the kids. And she made it even worse with a throwaway line about Claude Ryan's wife being one of those women…" This, in turn, led to a huge "No" rally of the Yvettes in the Montreal Forum.

The campaign going against him, a rattled René Lévesque also goofed, denouncing Trudeau, "His name is Pierre Elliott Trudeau and this is the Elliott side taking over, and that's the English side, so we French Canadians in Quebec can't expect any sympathy from him."

A scornful Trudeau responded that Elliott was not an English, but a Scottish name, "… Elliott was my mother's name. It was the name borne by the Elliotts who came to Canada more than two hundred years ago. It is the name of the Elliotts who, more than one hundred years ago, settled in Saint-Gabriel-de-Brandon, where you can still see their names on the tombstone in the cemetery. That is who the Elliotts are. My name is a Quebec name. But my name is a Canadian name also. And that's my name."

I first met René Lévesque for drinks in an East End Montreal restaurant in 1970. At the time, I took the chain-smoking, obviously high-strung Lévesque for an authentic people's tribune.

As I wrote in *Life*, he struck me as a man effortlessly in touch with the bookkeeper with sour breath, the wasting clerk with dandruff, the abandoned mother of five, in fact with all the discontented lives. Only later did I discover that the man had sides to him. On our first meeting, determined to dissociate the PQ from the FLQ, he denounced the latter group to me as "a bunch of bums." But seven years earlier, when the FLQ was given to planting bombs in mailboxes that could explode in the faces of children (a policy that, incidentally, obliged circumspect "Westmount Rhodesians" to send their Québécois pur laine or Caribbean maids out to mail the letters), Lévesque had said to André Laurendeau, "You've got to hand it to them, they're courageous, those guys."

In a couple of sizzling speeches delivered in Quebec City and Montreal, Trudeau ridiculed the referendum question, dubbing it the ultimate cowardice "because it does not have the courage to put a simple question, 'Do you Quebecers want to separate, yes or no?' Instead, having led Quebecers to the sovereignty well, it refused to drink the water." The PQ, Trudeau said, was ambiguously "asking you to say yes to a question that you can't honestly answer. They are asking you whether you want an association with other provinces, but how can your vote in Quebec force the other provinces to want to associate with you if you separate?" Later, the logician in him would toss in a spanner that the partitioners have made their own and that still rankles the separatists, "if Canada is divisible," he said, "so is Quebec."

On May 20, 1980, Quebecers voted 59.4 percent "NO" and 40.6 percent "YES." Trudeau, at his very best, did not gloat, but instead offered a grace note. He could not forget, he said, all those "YES" supporters who had fought with such strong conviction. "I am unable to rejoice without qualifications…. To my fellow Quebecers who have been wounded by defeat, I wish to say simply that we have all lost a little in this referendum. If you take account of the broken friendships, the strained family relationships, the hurt pride, there is no one among us who has not suffered some

Eighties Identity

U.S. President Ronald Reagan was elected in November 1980, less than a year after Trudeau's return to office. The two leaders differed in their economic and philosophic ideals. During Reagan's March 1981 inaugural visit to Ottawa (TOP LEFT), in the midst of escalating Middle East conflict, he offered a bemused Trudeau this rumination: "You have three kinds of peoples involved, right? There's the Jewish peoples. There's the Arab peoples. And then, there's us, the Christian peoples. And we're all God-fearing peoples, right? So why can't we just get together and fight the communists?"

Trudeau's fourth mandate found him back in the spotlight as the country's most eligible bachelor, appearing with some of the world's most beautiful women – among whom were classical guitarist Liona Boyd (TOP RIGHT) and actresses Barbra Streisand and Margot Kidder. Meanwhile, Terry Fox won the heart of the nation as he began his heroic Marathon of Hope

(MIDDLE RIGHT) in the summer of 1980. Fox's battle with cancer would take his young life a year later.

In response to the astronomical rise of international oil prices, Trudeau's 1980 National Energy Program ensured Ottawa's greater control over the production and distribution of oil and an equal price for all Canadian regions. Unsurprisingly, oil-rich Alberta (BOTTOM RIGHT) was fiercely opposed. After a year of intense negotiations, in September 1981 the federal government and Alberta Premier Peter Lougheed reached a compromise intended to increase oil revenues for both levels of government.

Fortunately for hosers Bob and Doug McKenzie – comedians Rick Moranis and Dave Thomas (BOTTOM LEFT) – the cost of oil had little impact on the price of beer and back bacon. In 1981 the comedy duo showcased its unique brand of Canadian nationalism in its first television episode of *The Great White North*.

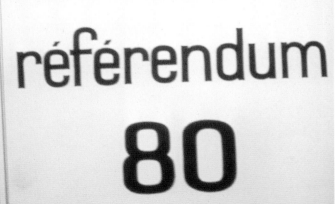

référendum 80

wound which we must try to heal in the days and weeks to come."

Trudeau next undertook to patriate Canada's Constitution, mouldering in Westminster, a task at which a number of previous prime ministers had failed. Backed by the premiers of Ontario and New Brunswick, Bill Davis and the late Richard Hatfield, he managed it in the end, but only at the cost of acrimony that is still with us. The PQ government, led by a seething René Lévesque, refused to sign on, claiming they had been betrayed by the Gang of Eight in a night of long knives. This has left us with the enduring myth that Quebec was not a party to the Constitution, which enabled Mulroney, years later, reading from a script written for him by one Lucien Bouchard, to say he would shuffle the furniture around with such élan, that Quebec would be able to sign on with honour.

However, the truth is that in November 1981, 71 of Quebec's 75 MPs supported Trudeau's constitutional package, as did a good many provincial Liberal MNAs and Mulroney himself, at the time. So, on April 17, 1982, the good Queen Elizabeth II signed the necessary papers, rendering Canada independent at last, in name as well as long-established fact.

Happy New Year, Joe Clark.

On January 2, 1983, even though he had won the support of two-thirds of the delegates at the convention in Winnipeg, Joe Clark stood down as Tory leader, but announced he would be a candidate in a leadership convention. Wiping tears from his eyes, Brian Mulroney began to make his moves, immediately winning the support of the PQ, as well as so-called "soft" nationalists, including Brian's cherished chum, Lucien Bouchard. Mulroney, promising the Tories he could deliver Quebec on a platter, which turned out to be true, was elected leader at the Tory convention in Ottawa on June 11, 1983. At the time, Mulroney came out strongly against a free-trade deal with the US, as opposed to John Crosbie,

another leadership candidate, but, as we all know, Mulroney later had second thoughts. Or grew in office. Whichever.

Then, on February 28, 1984, Pierre Elliott Trudeau took one of his long walks in the snow in Ottawa. "Sixteen years earlier," he wrote in his memoirs, "on a similar winter's walk, I had agonized over whether to stand for the leadership of the Liberal Party. My 1984 decision was easier to make. My three boys were entering their teens and I felt a need to spend more time with them. For all their lives until then ... they had been the prime minister's children, set apart from others by that fact, accompanied by bodyguards and so on. I wanted them to spend at least their teenage years as ordinary youngsters in Montreal, entirely away from public life. I also didn't know whether I had the energy left to fight another gruelling election campaign.... It was time to go home."

He announced his retirement the next morning.

PIERRE ELLIOTT TRUDEAU WAS ARROGANT. HE COULD be petulant. But, whatever his flaws, he was undoubtedly the greatest prime minister of our time. A true original. Not an untrustworthy, shallow charmer like Brian Mulroney. Or a political hack. Like Jean Chrétien. "He haunts us still," wrote Christina McCall Newman and Stephen Clarkson in their biography of Trudeau.

Most of all he haunts the Mulroneys.

One day Mila complained to a reporter that she couldn't fathom why the country was infatuated with the short, pockmarked man when her husband was such a handsome devil.

Much given to braggadocio, but basically insecure, Mulroney once confided in *Maclean's* how close he was to Bush père. Suggesting that Trudeau, in office, would not have been able to manage it, he said, "I can get George or Barb on the phone any time."

Yes, but only because Trudeau, a notorious skinflint, would probably have called collect.

Vote "No"

On May 20, 1980, Premier René Lévesque (TOP LEFT) held a provincial referendum on the right to negotiate Quebec's separation from Canada. Early in the campaign the separatist "Oui" contingent looked to be ahead of the province's federalist forces led by Quebec Liberal Leader Claude Ryan (BOTTOM LEFT), prompting Trudeau to instruct Justice Minister Jean Chrétien to "get in there a bit more vigorously" and to "play whatever role you want, because we're behind in the polls." By May 14, when Trudeau, Chrétien (BOTTOM RIGHT), and other leading Québécois politicians convened at Montreal's

overflowing Paul Sauvé Arena for an emotionally charged "Non" rally (TOP RIGHT), the federalists had mounted a convincing attack.

Trudeau delivered an impassioned forty-minute speech to the 10,000-strong rally. He countered Lévesque's ill-advised stab at his "English" middle name – it was his mother's Scottish name, actually, with 200-year-old roots in the province to boot – and accused the PQ of lacking the courage to put to its constituents what should have been a simple question: "Do you want to leave Canada, yes or no?" Trudeau went on to promise that upon a "Non" vote the

federal government would move immediately to renew the Constitution. With less than a week to go before the referendum, Trudeau's commitment to change swayed a significant number of Québécois to vote "Non."

It was René Lévesque's sovereignty-association pitted against Pierre Trudeau's Canadian federation, and on May 20, Quebecers made their decision: 40.6 percent in favour of separation, 59.4 percent against. Standing before disheartened supporters at the Paul Sauvé Arena, a shaken Lévesque vowed "À la prochaine!" (Next time!)

And one must say no to contempt, because they have come to that. I was told that … Mr. Lévesque was saying that part of my name was Elliott and, since Elliott was an English name, it was perfectly understandable that I was for the No side, because, really, you see, I was not as much of a Quebecer as those who are going to vote Yes. That, my dear friends, is what contempt is. It means saying that the Quebecers on the No side are not as good Quebecers as the others and perhaps they have a drop or two of foreign blood, while the people on the Yes side have pure blood in their veins … Of course my name is Pierre Elliott Trudeau. Yes, Elliott was my mother's name. It was the name borne by the Elliotts who came to Canada more than two hundred years ago. It is the name of the Elliotts who more than one hundred years ago settled in Saint-Gabriel-de-Brandon where you can still see their graves in the cemetery. That is what the Elliotts are. Mon nom est Québécois but my name is a Canadian name also and that's the story of my name.

PIERRE ELLIOTT TRUDEAU │ ADDRESS AT NO CAMPAIGN RALLY │ MAY 14, 1980

The Long Road

Trudeau began taking steps to patriate Canada's Constitution on May 21, 1980, the day after Quebec's referendum. On June 9, the premiers gathered at 24 Sussex Drive (FIRST ROW, LEFT) to discuss Trudeau's proposed strategy. They left the meeting (FIRST ROW, MIDDLE AND RIGHT) having given little heed to Trudeau's suggestion that he unilaterally seek permission from the British Parliament to patriate the Constitution.

Trudeau's next step was to visit London, where he left 10 Downing Street on June 25 (SECOND ROW, LEFT) after British Prime Minister Margaret Thatcher agreed to support his constitutional drive. Back in Canada, however, Trudeau faced further challenges. Although Joe Clark (SECOND ROW, MIDDLE) agreed with Trudeau's proposal, he was uncomfortable with the provinces' exclusion from the process. The Conservatives' March 1981 filibuster stalled the government legislation long enough to permit Newfoundland's Supreme Court to rule on March 31 against the legality of the Liberals' unilateral approach.

Newfoundland's decision forced the federal government to defend its position before the Supreme Court. After considerable protests from a number of interest groups, including Quebec's Saint-Jean-Baptiste Society (SECOND ROW, RIGHT), the court declared on September 28 that, although technically legal, the government's policy violated Canada's constitutional convention. Trudeau knew he had to attempt one final round of negotiations with the country's premiers.

On November 2, 1981, Trudeau (THIRD ROW, LEFT) and Canada's premiers – including Peter Lougheed and René Lévesque (THIRD ROW, MIDDLE) – and their constitutional experts (THIRD ROW, RIGHT), returned to the negotiating table. After two days of fruitless discussions (ABOVE), Trudeau suggested holding a national referendum. Turning to Lévesque, he said, "You're the great democrat. You're the great believer in referendums. You can't be opposed to one. Or are you afraid to take me on?" Relishing the prospect of another faceoff against the prime minister, Lévesque shot back, "Okay. I'd like to fight the Charter." Trudeau cracked the gavel and adjourned the morning's session.

Unwilling to relinquish their provincial powers and face a national referendum, the other nine provinces embarked on a flurry of negotiations with the federal government. On November 5, 1981, the conference ended in a deal – with every province but Quebec – to bring home the Constitution. While Trudeau, accompanied by advisers including Michael Kirby and Jean Chrétien, (FOURTH ROW) popped the cork off the champagne, back in Quebec City Lévesque fumed, "Trudeau m'a fourré" (Trudeau fucked me).

1982 | Canada's Constitution

Patriation

On April 17, 1982, Queen Elizabeth II and Prince Philip (TOP ROW, LEFT) mount the stage constructed on Parliament Hill for the signing of Canada's Constitution. With the first anxious onlookers arriving as early as 5:30 a.m., over 30,000 people (TOP ROW, RIGHT) would eventually brave the darkened Ottawa skies. Noticeably absent from the ceremonies was René Lévesque, who remained in Montreal to lead 20,000 protesters in a bitter march against the Constitution.

In Trudeau's speech to the assembled crowd (BOTTOM ROW, LEFT) he addressed Lévesque's non-appearance: "The government of Quebec decided that it [the Constitution] wasn't enough. It decided not to participate in this ceremony, celebrating Canada's full independence." Trudeau went on to defend his government's decision to proceed without Quebec's endorsement: "History will show, however, that nothing essential to the originality of Quebec has been sacrificed."

Trudeau beams as the Queen signs the Constitution (BOTTOM ROW, RIGHT) in the company of Privy Council Clerk Michael Pitfield (ON HER LEFT) and Secretary to the Cabinet for Federal-Provincial Relations Michael Kirby (ON HER FAR LEFT). In Elizabeth II's address she noted, "Although we regret the absence of the premier of Quebec, it is right to associate the people of Quebec with this celebration because, without them, Canada would not be

what it is today." Ironically, three of the four signatories – Justice Minister Jean Chrétien, Registrar General André Ouellet, and Prime Minister Pierre Trudeau – were French Canadian.

Queen Elizabeth and Trudeau (ABOVE) take a twenty-minute walk through the crowd after the historic signing of a Constitution now legal for the first time in both official languages. In it Trudeau had delivered the Charter of Rights and Freedoms, entrenching the fundamental freedoms, legal rights, and equality rights of all Canadians regardless of race, origin, colour, religion, sex, age, and disability.

East and West

On November 15, 1982, Pierre Trudeau (BELOW) attends the funeral of Soviet General Secretary Leonid Brezhnev in Moscow's Red Square. Succeeding Brezhnev was Yuri Andropov, former head of the Russian Committee of State Security (KGB), who set the tone for East-West relations only days after Brezhnev's death with this remark: "We know well that the imperialists will never meet one's pleas for peace. It can only be defended by relying on the invincible might of the Soviet armed forces." Mounting global tension spilled into Canada in early 1983 when the Liberal government reluctantly agreed to American cruise-missile testing in Canada.

A Korean mourns the death of his relative (OPPOSITE, BOTTOM), killed after Soviet forces shot down Korean airliner KAL 007 on September 1, 1983. The Soviets claimed that the plane, which had crossed into Soviet airspace over the Sea of Japan, was spying on a Russian military base. All 269 passengers and crew members, including ten Canadians, were killed. U.S.-Soviet tensions escalated after the incident, while for Trudeau, who months before had said "I was for peace before I entered politics and I'm not going to wait until I'm out before speaking out and trying to get things changed," the disaster only solidified his decision to begin a final crusade.

Into Office

Climbing the stairs of Parliament, Brian Mulroney (LEFT) leaves Question Period shortly after being elected leader of the Progressive Conservative Party on June 11, 1983. The Baie Comeau native – the first Quebec Tory leader in ninety-two years – was twenty years younger than his Liberal counterpart. As a law student at Quebec City's Laval University in the early 1960s Mulroney had attended a lecture given by a young Montreal law professor named Pierre Trudeau. Mulroney would later comment, "I was impressed with him as an intelligent man and an impressive individual, but not as a lawyer."

Around the World

On October 27, 1983, almost two months after the Korean airline disaster, Trudeau announced his intention to "devote our full political resources to reducing the threat of war." Some saw Trudeau's initiative as an about-face. Only a year before, in November 1982, Trudeau had driven a Leopard tank during a visit to the Canadian Forces Base in Lahr, West Germany (FIRST ROW, LEFT). And, sharply criticized throughout his leadership for his reluctance to support Canada's military, in his final mandate Trudeau had uncharacteristically increased defense spending by almost 82 percent. It wasn't the government's renewed commitment to Canada's conventional armed forces (FIRST ROW, MIDDLE) that drew the country's fire, but rather Trudeau's willingness to assist the U.S. cruise-missile program (FIRST ROW, RIGHT) by allowing its testing on Canadian soil.

In November 1983 Trudeau's peace initiative took him to Paris, The Hague, Brussels, Rome, The Vatican, and London, after which he set out for Tokyo (SECOND ROW, LEFT, MIDDLE, AND RIGHT), Dacca, New Delhi, and Beijing.

Before attending a Commonwealth conference in New Delhi Trudeau toured Bangladesh (THIRD ROW, LEFT) to a warm welcome (THIRD ROW, MIDDLE AND RIGHT). In January 1984 Trudeau visited Prague (FOURTH ROW), where he was greeted with a formal reception and a military honour guard. Although the Czech government allowed that Canada's initiative was "useful and correct," it condemned the deployment of American cruise missiles in Europe. Trudeau's subsequent visits to East Berlin and Bucharest – made after he had denounced NATO's nuclear strategy during an international conference in Davos, Switzerland (ABOVE) – met with a more positive reception.

The response of the superpowers to Trudeau's peace initiative was mixed: In December 1982, before returning to his own Strategic Defense Initiative (aka Star Wars), Reagan wished Trudeau "Godspeed in your efforts to help build a durable peace," while Soviet Foreign Minister Andrei Gromyko, amidst the turmoil of Andropov's death in February 1983, pronounced that relations could improve only after the West expressed its willingness to negotiate.

1984 | Resignation

Farewell

Trudeau resigned on February 29, 1984, sixteen years after first occupying the Prime Minister's Office (RIGHT). On June 14, two weeks before his last day as prime minister, over 8,000 members of the Liberal Party bade Trudeau farewell at the Ottawa Civic Centre (OPPOSITE), where supporters chanted his name and waved placards bearing his image. The celebration included a nationally televised tribute featuring performances by singer-songwriter Paul Anka and impersonator Rich Little. Film clips of famous events during the prime minister's tenure relived stirring moments from the 1968 campaign, the October Crisis, and Trudeau's journeys around the world.

In his *Memoirs* Trudeau wrote that he had left public life in order to spend more time with his sons, who "for all their lives until then, from the moment each of them was born ... had been the prime minister's children, set apart from others by that fact .... I wanted them to spend at least their teenage years as ordinary youngsters in Montreal." And, now almost sixty-five, Trudeau doubted whether he had the energy for the rigours of the campaign trail.

After carrying out his last acts in office – announcing 225 patronage appointments, among them Jeanne Sauvé as Canada's first woman Governor General; seeing to an array of final legislation in the House of Commons, including the Canada Health Act and the 1982 Young Offenders Act; and taking one final sojourn on the world stage at England's G7 Economic Summit in early June of 1984 – Trudeau's remarkable career had reached its completion.

The prime minister concluded his June 14 speech to the Liberal Party with these words: "Our hopes are high. Our faith in the people is great. Our courage is strong and our dreams for this beautiful country will never die." Joined by his three sons, Justin, Sacha, and Michel, Trudeau accepted a final wave of applause before exiting the stage.

The Sphinx
1984 to 2000

The Sphinx | Catherine Annau

I AM A CARD-CARRYING MEMBER OF THE TRUDEAU generation. Those of us born in the 1960s were too young to vote for Pierre Elliott Trudeau. All we got to do was grow up with him.

The way I see it, if the 1970s belonged to Trudeau and my optimistic adolescence, then the 1980s belonged to the men in dark suits and the reality of adulthood. Our new prime minister Brian Mulroney, speaking to bankers in New York City in 1984, declared that "Canada is now open for business" and enjoined the Big Boys to buy up the country. During the Mulroney years, venerable national institutions were dismantled or cut back to the bone. A new mantra of "privatization" and "deficit reduction" was chanted from sea to shining sea. The new guard informed us that we had been "overprotected" and that from now on we Canucks had to face the harsh realities of the real world.

But by the early 1990s our American conquerors, having snagged all the free toiletries and towels they could, checked out – leaving us to stumble through what were the worst economic times since the 1930s. Brian Mulroney, so confident and imperious early in his reign, now stood helplessly amid the wreckage of the Meech Lake and Charlottetown accords. Despite this would-be nation builder's best efforts to make his mark on history, the situation in Quebec had actually deteriorated. The place cards had been tossed, the chairs had been put on the tables and the party was definitely over.

The dismal climate of the early 1990s made it hard to remember that Canada hadn't always been this way. I grew up in Toronto in the 1970s, in what is now known as the heyday of Canadian nationalism. Both my parents were immigrants. My father left Hungary in 1945, just ahead of Stalin's legions, and came to Canada in 1951, the same year as my British-born mother. My parents met on a blind date in 1952. I came on the scene in 1965, with my two sisters following in 1968 and 1970. My childhood was a mosaic of cultural influences, from my Hungarian grandmother's hazelnut cookies to a well-worn collection of Enid Blyton's books to hanging out at the local mall.

Like many who had come before me, I searched for a Canadian identity. I found mine in Trudeau's vision of a Canada that was one country, two languages, many cultures. Looking back, I realize that Trudeau's idea of Canada was so pervasive it might have been an additive in our drinking water. Between the Participaction propaganda I was fed in elementary school, my French classes, and my parents' endless enthusiasm for the new Canada, I became a Trudeauite by osmosis. It may seem naïve, but it worked for me. It made a neat fit with my particular linguistic and cultural pedigree.

A thoroughly modern Canadian, I embraced learning French because for me a bilingual Canada *was* Canada. Only much later, in my thirties, did I come to realize how fully I had bought into Trudeau's vision. A keener I might have been, but I truly believed that learning to speak French was about saving the country.

Senior Counsel

Pierre Trudeau sits in his office at the downtown Montreal law firm Heenan Blaikie. Less than two months after his last official day as prime minister, the firm had announced that Trudeau was to be its newest counsel.

Following his retirement, Trudeau would also embark on numerous summer-long journeys around the globe – to France, the British Isles, South East Asia, China, Japan, and Serbia – accompanied by his sons. When in Montreal, Trudeau has enjoyed the city much as he did when he last lived there, twenty years earlier. Over the past fifteen years he has been spotted frequently – attending sporting events, skiing in the Laurentians, dining out with friends at the Ritz-Carleton. Those who find themselves in Trudeau's presence often stare in wonderment and occasionally exchange greetings. In October 1985, at his sixty-sixth birthday celebrations, Senator Philippe Gigantès remarked, "His muscles, when one pats his arm, are of iron. Girls turn to look at him admiringly in the street. His wit sparkles, as always. His grace and class are, as always, unparalleled."

At sixteen, I plastered the walls of my North Toronto bedroom with posters stolen off construction hoardings during visits to Quebec City and Montreal. The posters served as teen wallpaper, but they also reminded me of the romance and adventure of the exotic other world only a few hours down the road from boring Toronto. I spent hours lying on the living room floor of my girlfriend Gill's house, memorizing the lyrics to songs by Québécois folk-rockers Harmonium, smoking clove cigarettes, and blissfully dreaming of having a French-Canadian boyfriend.

So intoxicated were Gill and I by the promise of Québécois culture that we even took a vacation to Quebec City in the dead of winter. To sanctify the memory, I'd love to say this trip was when I met my French-Canadian dream lover. But the truth was anything but romantic. The weather was so cold we spent less time on the Plains of Abraham than the fifteen minutes the actual battle lasted, then spent two hours in a café just inside the walls of the old city desperately trying to warm up. The only men we met belonged to the middle-aged lonely-hearts crowd. Still, our dream of French Canada persisted.

In the midst of all my teenage angst, one thing was certain. P.E.T. was my hero, and there was no way the country was going to fall apart under his watch. So, for me, the 1980 referendum drama came and went without much surprise. In 1982, after Canada got its own Constitution, I remember my father coming home from Ottawa where he'd been on business, bearing gifts of constitutional memorabilia. He had booklets from the swearing-in ceremony, first-day-issue stamps, and copies of the Constitution Act for my sisters and me. I wasn't excited by these souvenirs so much as puzzled. By his own admission, my father had stumbled upon the ceremony

and scarcely seen it across the sea of heads and umbrellas on Parliament Hill. As for the document itself, which had been so long fought over and was, with its Charter of Rights and Freedoms, a truly magnificent achievement, it seemed somewhat underwhelming: a rather ugly bureaucratic booklet notable only for the bad design typical of so many government publications. The excitement around the 1980 referendum I had understood – the visuals were better; the ideas easier to grasp. This I could not. It wasn't until our geography became explicitly linked to constitutional accords that I began to sense that this poorly packaged document would prove to fascinate politicians far more than had the 1980 Referendum ever did.

In the fall of 1985, as I headed from Toronto to Montreal for my first year at McGill, the issue of separation seemed to me to be pretty much dead. And as politically inclined as I was, the prospect of finally living in the city I had so long idealized preoccupied me much more. Once there, I relished walking through the Plateau on my way to the university and hearing French being spoken all around me. Frustrated by my slow progress at speaking French, in the summer of 1988 I journeyed up to Chicoutimi to take part in the federal government's Second Language Bursary program. Politics seemed very far away as we watched French-Canadian movies and learned about French-Canadian culture and lived with French-speaking families. I even began to dream in French.

But in June 1990, still at McGill and now in the middle of my History M.A., I woke up. My buddies and I had decided to take in the annual Saint-Jean-Baptiste parade. Standing on the curb at Jeanne Mance and Sherbrooke, we watched as the colourful floats

New Beginnings

On June 16, 1984, sixteen years after his first attempt to gain the helm of the federal Liberal Party, a jubilant John Turner (TOP, SURROUNDED BY SUPPORTERS) won his party's leadership race. The front-runner heading into the convention, Turner defeated his closest opponent, Energy Minister Jean Chrétien, after the second ballot. Shortly after being sworn into office, Turner called an election for September 4, confident he could maintain the Liberal lead in the polls over Brian Mulroney's Conservatives. But after a series of campaign blunders, including a sportsmanlike pat on the rear of Liberal Party President Iona Campagnolo and two uninspired

television debates against Mulroney, John Turner's brief tenure as prime minister came to an abrupt halt. Brian Mulroney – who had promised to bring Quebec back into the Canadian fold with "honour and enthusiasm" – led the Conservatives to victory with 211 seats (fifty-eight in Quebec alone) in the House of Commons. The Liberals' twenty-one years in power had come to an end.

As the country embarked on a new political era, Margaret Trudeau briefly regained the national spotlight when she and her second husband Fried Kemper announced the birth of their first child, Kyle James Joachim

celebrating great moments in Quebec history gave way to chants of "Le Québec aux Québécois!" The air became, literally and metaphorically, stifling. As we drifted back to our apartments we felt like strangers in our own country, as if we were guest workers or tourists, and not particularly welcome ones at that. Upon graduation, fed up with a Canada that now promised neither economic nor political stability, many of my peers left to seek their dreams south of the border, in the country of cohesive myth and seemingly endless opportunity.

Where, I felt like screaming, was my Canada in all of this? Where was Trudeau's Canada, the dream I'd grown up believing in? And where was Trudeau himself? With his walk in the snow in 1984 – the one that took him all the way back to his Art Deco mansion in Montreal – we had lost a vision of ourselves as stylish and sophisticated. Meanwhile, the constitutional revisionists had blanketed the country in a profound sense of ennui. Occasionally, Trudeau would emerge to remind us of what we could be, what we might achieve, and what we were on the point of losing. With his accustomed flair he spoke out against Meech Lake, calling Mulroney and his companions "pleutres," and in the process sending the French and English media alike scurrying for their dictionaries. The old gunslinger showed he still had it. In 1992, at the eleventh hour, he issued a blistering attack on Charlottetown from the Montreal restaurant La Maison Eggroll, reminding us all that there was a larger vision at stake. He had not lost the ability to surprise and astonish us.

In 1995, Trudeau gave us perhaps the greatest surprise of all – he said nothing. Canada faced yet another Quebec referendum and the possibility of disintegration. Perhaps he was bullied into

(MIDDLE), in November 1984. The Kempers would later have a second child, Alicia, Margaret's first daughter.

In March 1985 Prime Minister Mulroney met with U.S. President Ronald Reagan on St. Patrick's Day in Quebec City, where the two leaders danced with their wives as they publicly crooned "When Irish Eyes Are Smiling" (BOTTOM). Mulroney – who had opposed free trade during the 1984 election campaign – worked out a free-trade agreement with the president, and in so doing reversed over a century of Tory orthodoxy that dated back to the National Policy of Canada's first prime minister, Sir John A. Macdonald.

silence by his political heirs who thought they could handle things, or perhaps he'd simply had enough. But those of us looking for someone to defend the country found the house lights down and the stage empty.

I can't emphasize enough how deeply the close call of 1995 shook me. In my mind I stood stunned amid the discarded "Oui" posters and "Non" balloons, the wrapping-paper remains of the second Quebec referendum in my lifetime. It felt like a bloodletting. This wasn't politics in the abstract; it was my home, my family, my neighbourhood that was at stake. My lovers, my friends, my trains, and my trails. It was the country of my parents' new beginnings, the country that had shaped me. This near-death experience, witnessed via television, galvanized me to begin work, first in my own head and by 1997 at the National Film Board, on what would become my film, *Just Watch Me: Trudeau and the 70s Generation*.

After graduation I had returned to Toronto, where through good luck and good timing I found myself working in film as a researcher. With hindsight, it seems obvious that I would one day make a documentary about bilingualism, Trudeau, and my generation. But at the time the subject didn't seem quite sexy enough, and I was too busy learning the ropes and paying my dues.

The promise of Trudeau's Canada, I realized, wasn't just part of my autobiography, it was the story of a whole generation of Canadians. Despite his contradictions and his failures, Trudeau encouraged us to believe in a Canada that was bilingual and multicultural, a nation that recognized French Canadians had suffered discrimination, and that sought to right those wrongs. He allowed us to see ourselves as an open, tolerant, intellectual, and romantic people. This is what I believed then and what I believe now, and no amount of smooth talking from men in dark suits is going to convince me otherwise.

I met Pierre Elliott Trudeau only once, and to tell the truth, it was something of a let down. The occasion was the Toronto relaunch of *Cité libre* in the winter of 1998. Since I had just begun the research for my NFB film, attending a reception with the man himself seemed propitious. So, on a cold, snowy, January evening my producer Gerry Flahive and I trekked down to Metro Hall. The room held a veritable Who's Who of the English-Canadian cultural and intellectual establishment – of about thirty years ago. At age thirty-two, I was perhaps the youngest person in the room and began to feel as if I'd crashed a bad party.

Suddenly klieg lights illuminated the podium, a receiving line was formed, and we all filed past the guest of honour. We were each given ten seconds to express our admiration and gratitude and get out of the way. My exchange with the Great Man was for all intents and purposes banal. He barely spoke and I was struck by how old and shrunken he seemed. A far cry from the last time I'd seen him on television, vigorously paddling a canoe. As I shook his hand, however, a slight smile crossed his lips and a distant twinkle could be discerned in his eyes. But there was no mistaking this for the Trudeau of my youth. That man had vanished. Like the era he had dominated.

Yet during those few brief seconds, I understood why Trudeau continues to captivate us. He showed us a Canada greater than the mere sum of its parts. His vision may have faded and the two solitudes may continue to divide us, perhaps now more than ever, but it still has the power to inspire us. I know this to be true, and I know Lucky Pierre knows it too. I saw it in his eyes.

At Home
Upon retiring from office, Trudeau returned to his Montreal Art Deco home (BOTTOM) built by the renowned French-Canadian architect Ernest Cormier in 1930. In December 1988, not far from the former prime minister's house, students protested the Supreme Court's unanimous ruling against Quebec's Bill 101 (ABOVE). The bill, which had banned all non-French commercial signage from storefronts, had been declared unconstitutional. Days later Quebec Premier Robert Bourassa overrode the Supreme Court's decision by invoking the Constitution's highly controversial Section 33, otherwise known as the "notwithstanding" clause. In a 1992 essay Trudeau predicted that future generations would cringe at Bourassa's decision, since "never before in the history of Quebec has a government suspended fundamental liberties to protect the French language and culture."

1987-89 | Calls for Unification

National Emergences

On April 30, 1987, Brian Mulroney and the country's ten premiers, including Ontario's David Peterson and Quebec's Robert Bourassa (BELOW), announced they had reached an agreement that would see Quebec accept the Constitution Act of 1982. The deal, known as the Meech Lake Accord, would address Quebec's various requests, including its bid for recognition as a "distinct society."

In late March 1988, a year after the signing the accord, Trudeau made a rare public appearance before a Meech Lake Senate hearing (RIGHT). A passionate opponent of national self-determination, Trudeau spoke out against the accord and its key promoter, Brian Mulroney, declaring that it was "not only bad in parts, it is all bad and should be put out in the dustbin."

Trudeau had opposed national self-determination throughout his adult life. In 1962 he wrote in *Cité libre*, "The tiny portion of history marked by the emergence of the nation-states is also the scene of the most devastating wars, the worst atrocities, and the most degrading collective hatred the world has ever seen."

Trudeau's words were prescient. In 1989 Soviet General Secretary Mikhail Gorbachev announced that the U.S.S.R. would no longer provide military support for neighbouring Communist governments, leading to the dismantling of the Berlin Wall that had divided the German city since World War II. On the morning of November 10, 1989, the most powerful symbol of the Cold War became an emblem of hope for hundreds of thousands of East Germans (OPPOSITE) who celebrated the start of new East-West relations. But Gorbachev's sweeping reforms and the breakup of the Soviet Union also paved the way for the re-emergence in the 1990s of bitter century-old nationalist voices in Eastern Europe. Nation-states would cry out for autonomy, and the world would witness the harrowing consequences of their struggle for self-determination.

From Oka to Charlottetown

On June 23, 1990, the deadline passed for ratification of the Meech Lake Accord after New Democratic Party MLA Elijah Harper, protesting the accord's failure to recognize aboriginals as a "distinct society" under the Constitution, refused to provide the unanimous consent necessary for Manitoba's ratification of the agreement.

Less than three weeks later, militant Mohawk Warriors (BELOW, AND OPPOSITE PAGE) in Oka, Quebec, demonstrated in a manner that made Harper's act of defiance look mild. Tensions between the Mohawks of Oka and Kahnawake and Quebec's provincial police force, La Sûreté du Québec, boiled over on July 11, 1990, after police efforts to overthrow the Mohawk barricade resulted in a three-hour exchange of gunfire that left one Quebec police officer dead. The Sûreté's use of violence provoked a number of aboriginal leaders to charge the Quebec government with seeking revenge against native groups for their role in dismantling the Meech Lake Accord. Alluding to the accord's recognition of Quebec as a "distinct society," Ovide Mercredi, vice-chief of the Assembly of First Nations, observed, "Quebec is distinct in its use of force against aboriginal people."

A second attempt to reform the Constitution came in August 1992, when Canada's leaders presented the Charlottetown Accord. In the weeks leading up to a national referendum on the accord, Pierre Trudeau once again entered the public eye when, in response to the desire of Quebec and of aboriginal Canadians for special status, he wrote: "If both are peoples and if people have the right to self-determination, what do you do about the problem of both these peoples inhabiting the same territory?" Trudeau added, "The claptrap of national self-determination must be discarded. What counts is improving the life chances of every Canadian, not protecting the abstract rights of 'peoples.'" The accord was defeated nationally by a narrow margin.

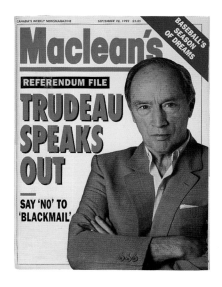

When all is said and done, the Canadian federation presupposes that, over and above our respective neighbourhoods, towns, cities, and provinces, Canada is considered to be the homeland of all Canadians. To avoid making a clear choice as Canadians (rather than as members of this or that province or city) by choosing to have feeble federal institutions would be to condemn ourselves to collective weakness in a world that will not be kind to nations divided against themselves. A country, after all, is not something you build as the pharaohs built the pyramids, and then leave standing there to defy eternity. A country is something that is built every day out of certain basic shared values. And so it is in the hands of every Canadian to determine how well and wisely we shall build the country of the future.

PIERRE ELLIOTT TRUDEAU | MEMOIRS | 1993

1995 | Referendum

Call for One Country

The failure of the Meech Lake Accord to receive provincial ratification in June 1990 led to a steady rise in support for Quebec's sovereignty movement. In September 1995 Quebec Premier and PQ Leader Jacques Parizeau announced that the province's second referendum on sovereignty-association would be held on October 30.

The campaign started out with the federalists consistently ahead in the polls, but the forces of secession gained momentum until, in the final weeks leading up to the referendum, it became unclear which side would win. On October 27, 150,000 people – many from across Canada – filled the streets of Montreal (BELOW, LEFT) in a massive display of national unity. In his address to the crowd, Prime Minister Jean Chrétien (BELOW, MIDDLE) declared, "We will be keeping open all the other paths for change. Including the administrative and constitutional paths." Chrétien's embrace of possible constitutional reforms highlighted the remarkable gains that sovereigntist leaders (BELOW, RIGHT) had made since the announcement of the referendum, when the prime minister had planned to avoid discussing constitutional change altogether. Yet despite the immense outpouring of emotion at the "Non" rally, the outcome of the October 30 referendum was far from certain.

Un Pays

After the demonstrators had tucked away their Canadian flags and bussed back to their home provinces, Quebec was left alone to decide whether its vision of one country included Canada. On October 30, 1995, a record number of Canadians crowded around their television sets to view the results of the referendum. When the final votes were counted, the federalists had won by a slim 50.6 percent to 49.4 percent. The dream of preserving one existing nation had almost died.

Days after the referendum Trudeau broke the silence he had maintained throughout the campaign, revealing that he had "sat on his hands" after federal strategists had suggested his active involvement was unnecessary. On February 3, 1996, Trudeau wrote an open letter to Parti Québécois Leader Lucien Bouchard, published simultaneously in Montreal's *La Presse* and *Gazette* newspapers. Trudeau accused Bouchard – who had led the "Oui" campaign during the final four weeks of the referendum – of having "betrayed the population of Quebec." The letter concluded: "By calling upon fallacies and untruths to advance the cause of hateful demagoguery, Lucien Bouchard misled the electors during last October's referendum. By his actions, he tarnished Quebec's good reputation as a democratic society and he does not deserve the trust of the people of this province."

1998 | Michel

In Memoriam

A well-versed outdoorsman, Michel, the youngest son of Pierre and Margaret Trudeau, had moved to Rossland, British Columbia, where he could enjoy the Canadian wilderness. Tragically, on the afternoon of November 13, 1998, the twenty-three-year-old Michel died in Kokanee Glacier Provincial Park (BELOW) when he was suddenly carried away to the centre of its deepest lake by an avalanche. Michel had been skiing with two companions. Another skier, who witnessed the tragedy unfold, later said, "We could see him….But we couldn't reach him." After a brief struggle with his restrictive clothing and hiking gear, Michel perished in the cold glacial waters.

As Canadians absorbed the news of the Trudeaus' loss, the former prime minister and his family (OPPOSITE, TRUDEAU, SACHA, MARGARET KEMPER, AND JUSTIN) mourned Michel at a memorial service held in Outremont's Saint-Viateur Church on November 20. In an address to the House of Commons on the same day, Liberal MP Clifford Lincoln said, "Words always seem feeble and inadequate comfort in the face of immense tragedies such as the sudden loss of Michel Trudeau. But in the measure in which they can bring solace, I know I am expressing the deep feelings of all parties in offering to Mr. Pierre Elliott Trudeau, Mrs. Margaret Kemper and Michel's brothers Justin and Sacha our most profound sympathy."

While speaking of the effects of the drowning on Trudeau, retired senator Jacques Hébert, a long-standing friend of the former prime minister, said, "The death of his son was overwhelming to him. It took away something that was irreplaceable." But, Hébert added, "He's not a man to let himself go, or wallow in depression. His strength of character and spirituality helped see him through it."

Pleasure and Surprise

Although by 1999 Trudeau had been out of office for fifteen years, his image, his words, and his legacy continued to have a tremendous impact on Canadians. In *Trudeau and Our Times*, Stephen Clarkson and Christina McCall wrote of the former prime minister, "More than Trudeau's liberal values lingered after he had gone. His intellectual brilliance, moral integrity, toughness of will, spiritual intensity, and physical prowess made him a model for many Canadians aspiring to excellence in politics and other fields."

The body of writing both on and by Trudeau has dominated the Canadian media for over three decades. On the eve of a new millennium, Canadians looked back on the twentieth century to assess its most significant historic events, personalities, and newsmakers. Pierre Elliott Trudeau was at the top of all lists. "Loved, loathed, admired and despised," declared the Canadian Press. "A bold and provocative politician whose arrogance alienated different regions in different ways, he is the country's most enigmatic personality." The news service announced that the former prime minister had been voted the Canadian newsmaker of the century. The poll, taken from 148 newspaper editors and broadcasters, placed Trudeau well ahead of the country's second most renowned newsmaker, Terry Fox. Placing third on the list was Trudeau's great rival, René Lévesque. In his eightieth year, Trudeau responded to the honour with a brief letter in which he wrote, "I am at once surprised and quite pleased with the information."

Contributors

Catherine Annau is the director of *Just Watch Me: Trudeau and the 70s Generation*, which won numerous prizes including the Genie for Best Feature Length Documentary, and the Best Canadian First Feature Award at the 1999 Toronto International Film Festival. Annau is also the producer of the international award-winning documentaries *Wisdom of the Heart* and *The Power Refugees*.

J.L. Granatstein taught Canadian history at York University from 1966 to 1995 and writes extensively on 20th Century Canada. He was co-author of *Pirouette: Pierre Trudeau and Canadian Foreign Policy* and co-editor of *Trudeau's Shadow: The Life and Legacy of Pierre Elliott Trudeau*.

Alison Gordon is an award-winning author of six books, five of them novels. She co-directed publicity for Pierre Elliott Trudeau's 1968 Liberal leadership campaign. Gordon has more than 20 years' experience in broadcasting and journalism.

Peter Gzowski has been, at various times, a newspaper reporter and editor, a writer and editor at *Maclean's* and other magazines, a broadcaster and an author. He is best known for his years as host of "Morningside" on CBC Radio. He is a Companion of the Order of Canada and is currently the chancellor of Trent University in Peterborough, Ontario.

Anne Kingston is an award-winning author and journalist who currently writes a column on contemporary culture for the *National Post*. Her book, *The Edible Man: Dave Nichol, President's Choice and the Making of Popular Taste* was the winner of the 1995 National Business Book Award. She is currently at work on a book investigating the role of the modern wife.

Mordecai Richler was born in Montreal. While he is best known as an award-winning novelist, he is also the author of the highly controversial *Oh Canada! Oh Quebec!*. Mr. Richler currently writes columns for *Saturday Night* and the *National Post*, and is a regular contributor to *The New Yorker* magazine.

Photo Sources

Every effort has been made to contact copyright holders. In the event of omission or error, the editor should be notified at Otherwise Inc., 356A Queen Street West, Toronto, Canada, M5V 2A2.

The following agency and archive names have been abbreviated:

ANQ: ARCHIVES NATIONALES DU QUÉBEC
CCA: CANADIAN CENTRE FOR ARCHITECTURE
CMCP: CANADIAN MUSEUM OF CONTEMPORARY PHOTOGRAPHY
CP: CP PICTURE ARCHIVE
CPA: CANADIAN PACIFIC ARCHIVES
CTA: CITY OF TORONTO ARCHIVES
MG: MONTREAL GAZETTE
MMM: MUSÉE MCCORD MUSEUM
NAC: NATIONAL ARCHIVES OF CANADA
PABC: PROVINCIAL ARCHIVES OF BRITISH COLUMBIA
PAC: PUBLIC ARCHIVES OF CANADA
PMO: PRIME MINISTER'S OFFICE
PAM: PICTURE ARCHIVES OF MANITOBA
TRL: TORONTO REFERENCE LIBRARY

Opening Pages

Opener Trudeau with camera: NAC PA-175917; **Title page** "Trudeau for Strong Government": NAC; **Copyright page** Woman looking at Trudeau posters: NAC; **Table of Contents page** (LEFT TO RIGHT) Trudeau in Italy: CP; Trudeau: NAC; Woman kissing Trudeau: NAC; Margaret making speech: NAC; Trudeau walking: NAC; Trudeau facing lake: NAC.

The Contrarian 1919-1947

p.8 Trudeau graduation portrait: NAC PA-115081; p.11 King and Queen of France: NAC; p.12 (CLOCKWISE FROM LEFT) Sir Wilfrid Laurier in car: CTA SC244-8224; Montreal street: MMM MP-1984-105.22; View from Quebec cottage: NAC PA-8747; p.14 (CLOCKWISE FROM LEFT) War veterans: CTA SC-244-736; Winnipeg Strike: PAM; Wounded soldiers: PAC PA 1679; p.16 (TOP TO BOTTOM) Boxing match: NAC PA-4159; Two boys on tricycle: ANQ P630, P65049; p.17 (LEFT TO RIGHT) Priest: ANQ P630 D47249, P1; Empty classroom: NAC C20532; p.18 (CLOCKWISE FROM LEFT) Airship: ANQ P428, S3, D6, P5; Capital movie theatre: Notman Archives; Camillien Houde and Lucill Dumont: Cinémathèque Québécoise; p.19 (CLOCKWISE FROM LEFT) Belmont park: ANQ P48,P10,486; Baseball game: NAC PA-151879; Service station: NAC PA-133371; p.20 Men on train: CTA SC 244-2181; p.21 Luxury ocean liner: CPA NS-22722; p.22 Trudeau in Italy: CP; p.23 (TOP TO BOTTOM) Nazi soldiers: Corbis; Hitler youth: Corbis; p.24 Camp Ahmek: Taylor Statten Camps; p.25 (TOP TO BOTTOM) Mackenzie King in Berlin: NAC PA-119013; Shooting the Rapids: NAC; p.26 (TOP TO BOTTOM) Trudeau graduation portrait: NAC PA-115081; University of Montreal: Gabor Szilasi; p.27 (TOP ROW, LEFT TO RIGHT) Woman on production line:

NAC PA-119766; Anti-Conscription rally: NAC PA-107909; Japanese-Canadian women: NAC C47390; (CENTRE) Navy convoys on St. Lawrence: ANQ P630,D528,P1; (BOTTOM ROW, LEFT TO RIGHT) Soldiers in Italy: NAC PA114482; Atomic bomb: Popper Foto, Northampton; p.28 Trudeau and friend in Paris: CP; p.29 (LEFT TO RIGHT) Jefferson Memorial: Frank Scherschel; Paris: NAC; London: James Riddell; p.30 (LEFT TO RIGHT) Israel: NAC PA-167285; Reflection of Taj Mahal: NAC PA-192114; p.31 Execution: Corbis; p.33 Trudeau in the Middle East: NAC PA-204509; p.34 Displaced child: NAC PA-204509; p.35 (TOP TO BOTTOM) Louis St. Laurent and Mackenzie King: CTA SC244-2198; Chicoutimi, Quebec: ANQ.

Into Power 1949-1968

p.36 Trudeau dodging newsmen: CP; p.39 Maurice Duplessis and Cardinal Paul-Émile Léger: NAC PA-159670; p.40 (CLOCKWISE FROM LEFT) Trudeau in suit: NAC PA-144330; Asbestos: NAC PA-115075; Miner's change room: NAC PA-115073; Claude Jodoin: PAC PA-137090; United Steelworkers of America: NAC PA-115801; Labour artist: NAC PA-124364; p.42 (LEFT TO RIGHT) Réne Lévesque in Korea: NAC C79008; Maurice "Rocket" Richard: Michel Gravel; Louis St. Laurent at meeting: NAC PA-206470; p. 43 (LEFT TO RIGHT) St. Lawrence Seaway opening: NAC PA-206474; Montreal diner: CMCP; p.44 Trudeau reading: NAC; p.45 (CLOCKWISE FROM LEFT) Two men near airplane: NAC; F.R. Scott with mushroom: NAC; Mackenzie River: NAC; Boat: NAC; p.46 Trudeau and Gérard Picard: NAC PA-137103; p.47 (TOP TO BOTTOM) Louis St. Laurent and reporters: NAC PA-206283; Diefenbaker and his cabinet: NAC PA-206484; p.48 Lesage campaign poster: NAC PA-117499; p. 49 (LEFT TO RIGHT) Trudeau and Hébert in China: CP; Great Wall of China: Two Innocents in China by Jacques Hébert and Pierre Elliott Trudeau; p.50 Diefenbaker and the Kennedys: CMCP 63-9342C, Ted Grant; p.51 (LEFT TO RIGHT) Nun at Dorval Airport: Gabor Szilasi; Beatniks kissing: NAC PA-163164; p.53 Trudeau: Don Newlands; p.54 Pro-Canadian flag rally: CMCP, NAC PA-136137; p.55 Réne Lévesque at Radio Canada: Guy Borrmans; p.56 Trudeau at microphones: NAC PA-117502; p.57 Anti-Pearson protestors: NAC PA-206473; p.58 (TOP TO BOTTOM) Women on Parliament Hill: NAC PA-185506; Trudeau, John Turner and Jean Chretien: NAC PA-117107; p.59 (LEFT TO RIGHT) Geodesic dome: George S. Zimbel, Stephen Bulger Gallery; Fight at Expo 1967: CP; p.60 Trudeau supporters: NAC; p.61 Gérard Pelletier, Jean Marchand, Mitchell Sharp and Trudeau: NAC PA-206327; p.62

(TOP ROW, LEFT TO RIGHT) Hellyer supporters: NAC PA-206328; Man reading: NAC PA-206323; (CENTRE ROW, LEFT TO RIGHT) Women rallying for Kierans: NAC PA-206329; Winters rally: NAC PA-206322; Paul Martin's rally: NAC PA-206325; (BOTTOM ROW, LEFT TO RIGHT) Turner rally: NAC PA-206318; Trudeau at victory rally: NAC PA-206324; p.63 Trudeau at rally: NAC.

Just Watch Me 1968-1974

p.64 Trudeau in "Mandrake the Magician" outfit: CP; p.67 (TOP TO BOTTOM) Trudeau at 24 Sussex Drive: CP; Trudeau chased by female admirers: CP; Trudeau behind Prime Minister's desk: CP; p.68 (LEFT TO RIGHT) Protestor dragged from Parliament: NAC PA-206608; Marshall McLuhan: CMCP; Hippies playing guitar: NAC PA-189360; (SECOND ROW, LEFT TO RIGHT) Trudeau supporters: NAC PA-180806; Woman kissing Trudeau: NAC; Trudeau shaking supporters' hands: PABC BA-0002; (THIRD ROW, LEFT TO RIGHT) Tank in street: Corbis; Death of Martin Luther King: Chameleon Photos; Execution of Viet Cong: NAC PA-156103; (BOTTOM ROW, LEFT TO RIGHT) Radio Canada puppets: NAC; Trudeau diving into pool: CP; p.70 Trudeau on election campaign: NAC; p.72 Saint-Jean-Baptiste Day parade protest: NAC PA-152447; p.73 (CLOCKWISE FROM LEFT) Trudeau at parade: CP; Citizens in costumes: Sam Tata; Trudeau at polling booths: NAC PA-206331; p.74 Swearing in ceremony: CP; p.75 (TOP ROW, LEFT TO RIGHT) Trudeau making speech: CP; Meeting in dining room at 24 Sussex: NAC PA-206334; Hippies on Parliament Hill: NAC PA-206472; (SECOND ROW, LEFT TO RIGHT) Pierre Berton: NAC PA-206468; George F. Davidson: NAC PA-206467; Adrienne Clarkson: NAC PA-206469; (THIRD ROW, LEFT TO RIGHT) Harold Cardinal: NAC PA-206466; Trudeau and Jean Chretien at Northern Affairs meeting: NAC PA-170161; Chief D.K. Dieter: NAC PA-206465; (BOTTOM ROW, LEFT TO RIGHT) Abortion law protestors: NAC PA-164027; Riots at Sir George Williams University: NAC PA-139988; Trudeau with John Lennon and Yoko Ono: NAC PA-110804; p.76 (LEFT TO RIGHT) Canadian military: NAC PA-206463; Soldier outside house: NAC PA-206464; p.77 (TOP TO BOTTOM) Body of Laporte: CP; Paul Rose and Jacques Rose arrested: CP; Trudeau at Laporte funeral: NAC PA-151863; p.79 Saint-Jean-Baptiste Day reveler: Gabor Szilasi; p.80 Trudeau and Margaret: CP; p.81 (LEFT TO RIGHT) Trudeau and Mademoiselle Marceau: NAC PA-205854; Trudeau and Barbra Streisand: CP; p.82 (TOP, LEFT TO RIGHT) Robert Stanfield: CP; David Lewis: CP; (BOTTOM) Youthful supporter: NAC PA-175935; p.83 (LEFT TO RIGHT) Napoleon: David, National Gallery

of Art, Washington D.C., Samuel H. Kress Collection; Trudeau and Team Canada: NAC PA-175935; p.84 (CLOCKWISE FROM LEFT) Trudeau in China: CP; Tai Chi demonstration: CP; Chinese opera: CP; p.85 (CLOCKWISE FROM LEFT) Portrait of Mao: CP; Admirers of Margaret: CP; Margaret in China: CP; p.86 (LEFT, TOP TO BOTTOM) Trudeau at Western Conference: NAC PA206447; Réne Lévesque: NAC PA-115039; (RIGHT) Peter Lougheed: CP; p.87 Saudi leaders: Robert Azzi/Woodfin Camp.

Domestic Malaise 1974-1980

p.88 Trudeau at microphones: NAC PA-175947; p.91 Margaret making speech: NAC; p.92 (CLOCKWISE FROM LEFT) Keith Davey: NAC PA-115170; Jim Coutts: NAC PA-108134; Trudeau with supporters: NAC; p.94 (LEFT TO RIGHT) Liberal Convention: NAC PA-206471; Nixon and Trudeau: NAC; Morgentaler: NAC PA-132340; p.95 (LEFT TO RIGHT) Margaret Atwood: CMCP; Trudeau and Bourassa: NAC PA-206592; Margaret with camera: CP; p.96 Trudeau family portrait: NAC; p.97 Poor PEI family: NAC PA-206604; p.98 (LEFT TO RIGHT) CN rail lines: Jean Lauzon; Hydro plant: CMCP; p.99 (CLOCKWISE FROM LEFT) Woman protestor: Pierre Gaudard; Trudeau playing baseball: NAC PA-115163; MP All Stars: NAC PA-206598; Trudeau putting on shirt: NAC PA-2065999; p.100 Trudeau and Margaret with Castro: NAC; p.101 Trudeau fans in Cuba: NAC; p.102 (CLOCKWISE FROM TOP) Joe Clark being interviewed: NAC PA-206452; Parti Quebecois supporters: Daniel Kieffer, Group Zone; Saskatchewan farmers protest: CP; p.103 Trudeau, Margaret and Sacha: CP; p.104 Trudeau at Olympics: NAC PA-206518; p.105 Wrestling at Olympics: NAC PA-206520; p.106 Trudeau at Buckingham Palace: NAC; p.107 Margaret smoking: CP; p.108 SunLife building for sale in Montreal: CMCP; p.109 Ayatollah in Iran: Keler/C orbis Sygma; p.110 Trudeau at debate: NAC; p.111 (LEFT, TOP TO BOTTOM) Coutts: NAC; Davey and his wife: NAC; Liberal supporters: NAC; (RIGHT) Margaret at Studio 54: CP; p.113 Trudeau bust: Ken Elliott; p.116 (LEFT TO RIGHT) Trudeau in convertible: CP; Trudeau with beard: CP; p.117 (TOP TO BOTTOM) Réne Lévesque on TV: CP; Diefenbaker funeral train: CP.

I'm Back 1980-1984

p.118 Trudeau and sons: NAC PA-184566; p.121 Trudeau walking: NAC; p.122 Trudeau and Reagan: NAC; Lionna Boyd: NAC; Terry Fox: CP; Oil rig: NAC PA-206766; Bob and Doug McKenzie: SCTV; p.124 (CLOCKWISE FROM LEFT) Lévesque speaking: NAC; "Non" rally: NAC; Trudeau and Chretien at "Non" rally: NAC; Claude Ryan at "Non" rally: NAC; p.127

Trudeau at "Non" rally: NAC; p.128 (TOP ROW, LEFT TO RIGHT) Lévesque and Davis: NAC; Trudeau and Lougheed being interviewed: NAC; Lévesque and Trudeau being interviewed: NAC; (SECOND ROW, LEFT TO RIGHT) Thatcher and Trudeau: NAC; Joe Clark on telephone: NAC PA-206771; Saint-Jean-Baptiste Society demonstrating: CP; (THIRD ROW, LEFT TO RIGHT) Trudeau with binder: NAC PA-201934; Peter Lougheed and Réne Lévesque: NAC PA-201937; Constitutional Conference: NAC PA-201942; (BOTTOM ROW, LEFT TO RIGHT) Chretien in embrace: NAC PA-201947; Chretien uncorking champagne: NAC PA-201955; Trudeau with champagne: NAC PA-201960; p.129 Trudeau at Constitutional Conference: NAC; p.130 (CLOCKWISE FROM LEFT) Constitution ceremony in Ottawa: NAC; Crowd at ceremony: NAC; Queen Elizabeth: NAC; Trudeau at podium: NAC; p.131 Trudeau with Queen Elizabeth: NAC; p.132 Trudeau in Moscow: NAC PA-140294; p.133 (TOP TO BOTTOM) Brian Mulroney: NAC; Korean Airline mourners: Corbis; p.134 Trudeau on screen: NAC; p.135 (TOP ROW, LEFT TO RIGHT) Trudeau in tank: NAC; Helicopter: NAC; Cruise protestors: NAC; (SECOND ROW, LEFT TO RIGHT) Trudeau in Japan: NAC; Trudeau with officials: NAC; Trudeau on TV: NAC; (THIRD ROW, LEFT TO RIGHT) Trudeau in Bangladesh: NAC; Painting of Trudeau: NAC; Bangladeshis waving: NAC; (BOTTOM ROW, LEFT TO RIGHT) Prague skyline: NAC; Trudeau in Prague: NAC; Soldiers in Prague: NAC; p.136 Trudeau in Parliament Hill office: CP; p.137 Trudeau applauded: CP.

The Sphinx 1984-2000
p.138 Trudeau facing lake: NAC; p.141 Trudeau at Heenan Blaikie: J.M. Carisse; p.143 (TOP TO BOTTOM) Turner at rally: NAC; Margaret with new baby: CP; The Mulroneys and the Reagans: CP; p.144 (TOP) Quebec Bill 101: CP; (BOTTOM, LEFT TO RIGHT) Ernest Cormier's house, exterior: CCA AR01 P-6727; Interior of Cormier's House: CCA AR01 P-6744; p.146 (LEFT TO RIGHT) Mulroney, Peterson and Bourassa: CP; Trudeau at Meech Lake Accord: CP; p.147 Fall of Berlin Wall: Stephane Duroy/Agence Vu, Paris; p.148 Oka fight: NAC; p.149 Oka standoff: Robert Fréchette; CP; Mulroney with premiers: PMO; p.151 Trudeau in fringe jacket: Les Productions La Fête/John Demers; p.152 (LEFT TO RIGHT) Flag and crowd: MG; Chretien at microphone: MG; Rally: MG; p.153 "Un pays" sign: Serge Clément; p.154 Lake: CP; p.155 Michel Trudeau funeral: CP; p.157 Trudeau portrait: Charles Pachter.

Closing page
Trudeau on boat: NAC PA-201083.

Literary Sources
p.32 Pierre Elliott Trudeau, *Against the Current: Selected Writings 1939-1996* edited by Gérard Pelletier, McClelland & Stewart Inc.; p.52 Pierre Elliott Trudeau, *The Essential Trudeau* edited by Ron Graham, McClelland & Stewart Inc.; p.78 Pierre Elliott Trudeau, as cited in the *Toronto Star*, OCTOBER 17, 1970; p.112 Pierre Elliott Trudeau, as cited in the *Winnipeg Free Press*, MAY 23, 1979; p.126 Pierre Elliott Trudeau, as cited in *Trudeau and Our Times: The Magnificent Obsession* by Stephen Clarkson and Christina McCall, McClelland & Stewart Inc.; p.150 Pierre Elliott Trudeau, *Memoirs*, McClelland and Stewart Inc.

Sources Consulted
Towards a Just Society: The Trudeau Years. Edited by Thomas S. Axworthy and Pierre Elliott Trudeau. Translated by Patricia Claxton. TORONTO: PENGUIN BOOKS, 1992.

Clarkson, Stephen, and Christina McCall. *Trudeau and Our Times.* Vol 1, *The Magnificent Obsession.* TORONTO: MCCLELLAND AND STEWART, 1990.

—. *Trudeau and Our Times.* Vol 2, *The Heroic Delusion.* TORONTO: MCCLELLAND AND STEWART, 1994.

Trudeau's Shadow: The Life and Legacy of Pierre Elliott Trudeau. Edited by Andrew Cohen and J.L. Granatstein. TORONTO: RANDOM HOUSE OF CANADA LIMITED, 1998.

Granatstein, J.L., and Robert Bothwell. *Pirouette: Pierre Trudeau and Canadian Foreign Policy.* TORONTO: UNIVERSITY OF TORONTO PRESS, 1990.

Gwyn, Richard. *The Northern Magus: Pierre Trudeau and Canadians.* TORONTO: MCCLELLAND AND STEWART, 1980.

Kingwell, Mark, and Christopher Moore. *Canada Our Century.* TORONTO: DOUBLEDAY CANADA, 1999.

Laurendeau, André. *André Laurendeau: Witness for Quebec.* Translated by Claude Ryan. TORONTO: MACMILLAN COMPANY OF CANADA, 1973.

Lévesque, René. *René Lévesque: Portrait of a Québécois.* TORONTO: GAGE PUBLISHING LTD., 1975.

McKenna, Brian, and Susan Purcell. *Drapeau.* Clarke, IRWIN AND COMPANY LTD., 1980.

McLuhan, Marshall. *Letters of Marshall McLuhan.* Selected and Edited by Matie Molinaro, Corinne McLuhan, and William Toye. TORONTO: OXFORD UNIVERSITY PRESS, 1987.

Trudeau, Pierre Elliott. *Trudeau: A Mess that Deserves a Big No.* TORONTO: ROBERT DAVIES PUBLISHING, 1992.

—. *Memoirs.* TORONTO: MCCLELLAND AND STEWART, 1993.

—. *Against the Current: Selected Writings 1939–1996.* Edited by Gérard Pelletier. TORONTO: MCCLELLAND AND STEWART INC., 1996.

—. *The Essential Trudeau.* Edited by Ron Graham. TORONTO: MCCLELLAND STEWART, 1998.

Vigod, Bernard L. *Quebec Before Duplessis: The Political Career of Louis-Alexandre Taschereau.* MCGILL-QUEEN'S UNIVERSITY PRESS, 1986.

Periodicals Consulted
Anderson, Ian, "Cement For A Nation," *Maclean's*, 16 NOVEMBER 1981.

Bain, George, "A Prospective Candidate," *Globe and Mail*, 27 DECEMBER 1967.

Beirne, Anne, "The Few Who Stayed Out in the Cold," *Maclean's*, 26 APRIL 1982.

Bliss, Michael, "A Tattered Legacy," *Globe and Mail*, 16 OCTOBER 1999.

Booth, Amy, "Trudeau Brings 'A Perspective' to Law Firm," *Financial Post*, 29 SEPTEMBER 1984.

Came, Barry, "We the People," *Maclean's*, 18 SEPTEMBER 1995.

"Canada: Man of Tomorrow," *Time Canada*, 5 JULY 1968.

Caragata, Warren, "Back From the Brink," *Maclean's*, 6 NOVEMBER 1995.

Collins, Don, "Signing Ushers in New Canadian Era," *Ottawa Citizen*, 17 APRIL 1982.

—, "Ceremonies Leave PM in a Whirl," *Ottawa Citizen*, 19 APRIL 1982.

"Coming Along Slow But Fast," *Time Canada*, 31 OCTOBER 1969.

"Dear Pierre," *Saturday Night*, SEPTEMBER 1987.

"Debate That Never Was, The," *Time Canada*, 30 OCTOBER 1972.

Editorial, "A Bold New Program That Touches Us All," *Globe and Mail*, 23 DECEMBER, 1967.

Editorial, "Trudeau: The Boldest Reformer of Them All," *Toronto Star*, 22 DECEMBER, 1967.

"Ending a Strange, Indecisive Campaign," *Time Canada*, 8 JULY 1974.

Fox, Bill, "PM Pledges Quick Reform for Quebec," *Toronto Star*, 15 MAY 1980.

Fraser, Blair, "Who'll Be Around After the Battle?," *Maclean's*, 1 NOVEMBER 1965.

Fremon, Celeste, "Margaret Trudeau: The Story of the Rise (And the Many Falls) of Canada's Ex-First Lady," *Playgirl*, SEPTEMBER 1979.

Geddes, John, "A Life of Its Own," *Maclean's*, 19 JUNE 2000.

Gessell, Paul, "Life After 24 Sussex," *Maclean's*, 25 NOVEMBER 1985.

Goar, Carol, "The Trail from Baie Comeau to the Top," *Maclean's*, 20 JUNE 1983.

—, "The Mulroney Challenge," *Maclean's*, 20 JUNE 1983.

—, "Assessing the Peace Mission," *Maclean's*, 13 FEBRUARY 1984.

—, "Trudeau Goes to Moscow," *Maclean's*, 20 FEBRUARY 1984.

—, "Turner Faces the Future," *Maclean's*, 25 JUNE 1984.

Gzowski, Peter, "Angry Young Canadiens: Portrait of an Intellectual in Action," *Maclean's*, 24 FEBRUARY 1962.

Hay, John, "Assessing Trudeau's Plan," *Maclean's*, DECEMBER 26, 1983.

Honderich, John, "It Takes Courage to Vote No, PM Says," *Toronto Star*, 8 MAY 1980.

Iglauer, Edith, "Profiles: Prime Minister/Premier Ministre," *The New Yorker*, 5 JULY 1969.

Janigan, Mary, "Turner's Days of Decision," *Maclean's*, 25 JUNE 1984.

Laver, Ross, Bruce Wallace, and Lisa Van Dusen, "The Signs of Hostility," *Maclean's*, 26 DECEMBER 1988.

"Lennon and Yoko Meet PM: 'He's a beautiful man of peace'," *Toronto Star*, 24 DECEMBER 1969.

Lepage, Guy, "PQ Faithful Rally Against Constitution," *Ottawa Citizen*, 17 APRIL 1982.

"Lévesque Leading March Against Constitution," *Ottawa Citizen*, 17 APRIL 1982.

Lewis, Robert, and Susan Riley, "An Era Ends," *Maclean's*, 3 DECEMBER 1979.

—, "Canada Faces the 'Non' Challenge," *Maclean's*, 26 MAY 1980.

—, "An Act of Pride," *Maclean's*, 14 DECEMBER 1981.

—, "Rebirth of a Nation," *Maclean's*, 26 APRIL 1982.

"Liberals: A Man Who Demands Risks, The," *Time Canada*, 12 APRIL 1968.

MacDonald, Dan, "Trudeau and Lesage a Tough Act to Follow," *Montreal Gazette*, 9 MAY 1980.

Mader, William, and Peter Rehak. "Calgary Conference: The Door Opens," *Time Canada*, 6 AUGUST 1973.

McDonald, Marci, "Trudeau's Challenge to NATO," *Maclean's*, 26 NOVEMBER 1984.

O'Hara, Jane, "A Tribute to the Trudeau Legacy," *Maclean's*, 25 JUNE 1984.

—, "Heady Days", *Maclean's*, 6 APRIL 1998.

Peritz, Ingrid, " Trudeau at 80: In Twilight, He Still Stands Out. Age Has Slowed Him, But Pierre Trudeau Remains Sharp, Dignified and Fascinating," *Globe and Mail*, 16 OCTOBER 1999.

Phillips, Andrew, "Change Must Come if Vote's a No, PM Tells Rest of Canada," *Montreal Gazette*, 15 MAY 1980.

—, "The Choice In Quebec," *Maclean's*, 30 OCTOBER 1995.

"PM: Constitution a Fresh Beginning," *Ottawa Citizen*, 19 APRIL 1982.

"PQ Renews Drive for Separatism," *Ottawa Citizen*, 19 APRIL 1982.

"Quebec: A Brutal Escalation," *Time Canada*, 19 OCTOBER 1970.

"Queen Elizabeth: 'I Have Seen the Vision of this Country Take Shape'," *Ottawa Citizen*, 19 APRIL 1982.

Sclanders, Ian, "Ten Million Voters in Search of an Issue," *Maclean's*, 1 NOVEMBER 1965.

"Second Life of P.E.T., The," *Time Canada*, 13 NOVEMBER 1972.

Stevens, Geoffrey, "Bill Overhauls Criminal Code," *Globe and Mail*, 22 DECEMBER 1967.

Stewart, Walter, "Why They Can't Burst the Trudeau Balloon," *Maclean's*, JANUARY 1969.

Taylor, Greg W., Ann McLaughlin, and Bruce Wallace, "The Battle of Oka," *Maclean's*, 23 JULY 1990.

Thomas, Davis, "The Fear Merchants," *Maclean's*, 12 MAY 1980.

—, "'Non'-What Now?," *Maclean's*, 26 MAY 1980.

Trudeau, Pierre Elliott, "Trudeau Speaks Out," *Maclean's*, 28 SEPTEMBER 1992.

—, "I accuse Lucien Bouchard of Having Betrayed the Population of Quebec," *Montreal Gazette*, 3 FEBRUARY 1996.

"Very Special Chemistry, A," *Time Canada*, 9 FEBRUARY 1976.

"Voyage of Self-Discovery, A," *Time Canada*, 5 JULY 1968.

Wallace, Bruce, "Storm Over Meech Lake," *Maclean's*, 11 APRIL 1988.

Wallace, Bruce, Ross Laver, and Lisa Van Dusen, "War Over Words," *Maclean's*, 2 JANUARY 1989.

White, Scott, "Trudeau Named Canadian Newsmaker of the Century," *Canadian Press*, 6 DECEMBER 1999.

Wilson-Smith, Anthony, "The Struggle Begins," *Maclean's*, 18 SEPTEMBER 1995.

—, "A House Divided," *Maclean's*, 6 NOVEMBER 1995.

—, "The Lion in Winter," *Maclean's*, 6 APRIL 1998.

—, "The Day that Changed Canada," *Maclean's*, 19 JUNE 2000.

Winsor, Hugh, "A Tattered Legacy," *Globe and Mail*, 16 OCTOBER 1999.

Wood, Chris, "A Passionate Warning: Pierre Trudeau Lashes Out At Meech Lake," *Maclean's*, 12 MARCH 1990.

"Young Chieftain, The," *Time Canada*, 1 MARCH 1976.